Programme Planning in the Cub Scout Pack

The Scout Association
Baden-Powell House
Queen's Gate
London SW7 5JS

Programme Planning in the Cub Scout Pack

Written by:
Hazel Addis
Audrey Milan

Editorial:
T. A. Stringer
P. G. Brooks
General Editor:
Ron Jeffries

Illustrated by:
Peter Harrison

ISBN 0 85165 107 0

First Edition First Printing
August 1975

Fifth Printing
November 1983

Printed in Great Britain by
Whitstable Litho Ltd., Whitstable, Kent

CONTENTS

PART 1
Planning

'WHAT are we going to do tonight, Akela?'
There is so much anticipation and excitement in the question which is a challenge to any Cub Scout Leader at any Pack Meeting. But if Akela is also wondering: 'What on earth are we going to do tonight?' the challenge is apt to produce a sense of panic, calling for evasive action, which will probably result in disappointment for everybody at the end of the evening. Both from the Cub Scouts' point of view, with their need for immediate satisfaction, and for the leaders' overall aims, it is absolutely essential to know exactly what we intend to do and how we are going to do it.

The success of any Pack is entirely dependent on its programmes and how they are put over, and this is dependent on the time, care and know-how that goes into planning them. The material is there: the boys, ready and willing to do anything, whether it be a new activity or an old favourite, the development of an established interest or a complete surprise.
The means are there: Cub Scouting, with the tremendous scope and opportunity which has been devised and developed through the years, and yet is sufficiently elastic to meet all needs and suit all customers.
It is the leader's job to put these two factors together in the best possible way—programme planning.

Why is it necessary?

It is so easy to get into a rut, to drift along aimlessly and get nowhere. Boys are mercurial: they can get bored and disillusioned almost as quickly as they blaze up with enthusiasm.

If we waste time and miss opportunities, for lack of forethought, we are responsible for letting that enthusiasm fizzle out, leading to a loss of interest in the whole of Scouting, which might well have become a long-term interest and a way of life.

What is needed?

Time and method which can only be supplied by you, the Cub Scout leader, and, of course, the know-how and skills which are supplied by Leader Training.

Time

It is entirely up to you to decide how much time you can give to Scouting, taking due account of the priorities of your family and your job, or any other commitments or interests which may be necessary to keep you reasonably sane. But it is no good pretending that successful Cub Scouting will only occupy you for the time of the weekly Pack Meeting. And it is wrong to recruit others on this false premise. Good planning often takes nearly as long as the activity itself. But much of the pre-planning can be done on the bus or train, washing-up, shaving or having a hair-do. After that of course it must be put on paper, not just scribbled on the back of an envelope, but legibly and logically worked out, as a business-like briefing for the team.

Paper-work takes time; the acquisition of bright ideas may take ages!

Method

There are many methods of programme planning, just as there are many people who have no method at all. You may have your own, which seems to work well enough, or perhaps it might be open to improvement, especially if you analyse your difficulties and ask yourself why things didn't work out quite as you had hoped. It is easy to blame circumstances or the boys or the weather, but sometimes it may be your method of planning which needs a bit of an overhaul. It is a sobering thought that the older anything gets, the more frequently an overhaul is needed.

This book is designed to save you time, by collecting and collating the material, assessing the possibilities, and suggesting some methods of putting them over.

The skills

These you acquire through your training, and will practise and perfect by trial and error, keeping up to date by attending local events, exchanging ideas with other people and also by reading. Too many people make the mistake of thinking that the things they did on various training courses, fun as they were, don't really apply to *their* Pack, because it is different and nobody really understands it but themselves. Everybody's Pack is different and you should certainly know your own better than anybody else. Training is planned (with years and years of programme planning behind it!) to help everybody, but obviously adaptations are necessary to suit the individual. It is the idea and the object behind the idea which matter, and these can usually be adapted for town or country Packs, suburban, new estate, truly rural, or even yours which is probably quite different!

Equally it is true that the game you learned on your training course is not the only one of its sort which is recommended and you should not wear it threadbare. Each game or activity is only a sample of one particular aspect of our work; books and your own imagination can provide the variety which is essential. This is where your special knowledge of your own boys is all important, just as a wise Mum knows how to cater for her family, giving them all the necessary vitamins and proteins, but cooked and served in just the appetising way they like.

And the proof of the pudding is always available to Cub Scout leaders, for Cubs are completely honest and outspoken, sometimes devastatingly so; and tact, with all its complications, is gloriously unknown to them.

How to set about it?

First we must fix our overall aims by deciding what the boys want to do and what we think they ought to do. They should enjoy both these equally, indeed they shouldn't ever know which came under which category. Our objectives must be clearly established in our own minds, and on paper, before we can decide on our methods of putting them over.

Overall aims

1 Physical — exercising bodies and senses
2 Mental — establishing fresh interests and stimulating creativity
3 Spiritual/moral — developing character and personal values
4 Social — fitting boys for the society into which they are growing

All these may seem too obvious to be worth mentioning, but we do sometimes lose sight of them when we get bogged down in detail.

What the boys want

They want to make a noise; to enjoy the physical exhilaration of running, chasing about and letting off steam; to have fun, whatever they are doing.

Youngsters also have their quieter moments, and will give

their rapt attention for quite a long time to something which really intrigues them.
But boys are individuals and it is dangerous to generalise. As Cub Scout leaders we should get to know our boys really well, and should try to cater for the needs and characteristics of each individual. Leaders should neither attempt nor desire to turn out a uniform product. There are always one or two 'odd men out', who are just as important as the majority, maybe more so. Our programmes need to be immensely diversified, providing the occasional activity which will be most enjoyed by the few, although they will provide fresh opportunities for the many.
The old saying that the devil finds work for idle hands is all too often proved to be true in the Pack. If our programmes are not planned with every one of the boys in mind, some will get bored and will find their own sources of amusement, which may not amuse Akela at all.

What the boys need

As a general guide, they need what they want, like the puppy who chews coal because instinct tells him that he needs the minerals; the kitten who plays with a cotton-reel without realising that it is good training for mouse-catching. But they also do it because it is fun and they don't know when to stop. So perhaps this aspect of demand and supply is not quite so simple as it sounds; we have to give them what they need in reasonable portions, and exercise proper control over the things they want to do. We also aim to supply the growing mind and body with things which they didn't know they wanted. We have to remember too that the boys are constantly developing and changing, and what they enjoy at 8 years old may well be 'old hat' at 8½. Six months is a large slice of life for a child. We must be sensitive to the subtle changes that occur as the boys grow up. As leaders we must also keep the balance between the challenge we present to boys and their ability to achieve it.

What are we going to do?

We have to provide programmes for each Pack Meeting, skilfully mixing and balancing the right ingredients with:
variety, *to keep the boys on their toes;*
continuity, *to ensure steady development and all-round progress;*
lots of fun, *but with a purpose in everything we do;*
and of course any amount of imagination, in order to meet the requirements of everybody.

The ingredients

A proportion of each of these should be included in every Pack Meeting:

Work—*by using the Arrow Scheme or Proficiency badges, in order that something should be learned or something accomplished.*

Physical activity—*through games or strenuous activities.*

Sense training—*through games and other activities.*

Imagination and inspiration—*by means of yarns, camp fires and prayers.*

Discipline—*training in self-control, orderliness and the capacity for co-operation.*

Fun—*last but by no means least.*

To provide all these things for every boy at every Pack Meeting is quite a tall order. Let us have a closer look at them.

Work

There is no doubt that boys want to feel they are getting on. However small the achievement, they should be able to go home with a sense of satisfaction and more confidence for the next challenge.

Physical activity

What tremendous possibilities for variety lie in games alone, if we ensure that each one is a different type from the last. Physical activity may be the primary consideration but there is usually some other purpose, even if it is only the co-ordination of body and brain, mind and muscle. Many games provide an opportunity to practise Arrow skills in ways which are fun.

Sense training

Sometimes we are apt to think that because we were fortunate enough to be born with five senses they are ours for ever and will grow with us, like the five fingers on one hand. But if we never used or exercised one of those fingers it would probably become atrophied. Likewise these God-given attributes should not be neglected or even taken for granted—each one of them can provide a different form of delight.

Imagination

This is another sadly neglected gift in too many adults. At Cub Scout age it flourishes and it is up to us to keep it nourished (and maybe, even pruned!) and developed into a healthy state which will be the source of endless fun. Often it is the imaginative activities of boyhood days which are remembered all a man's life. It follows that the Cub Scout leader must be capable of triggering off the boys' imagination. An occasional surprise item may enliven the whole programme, but it calls for a lot of planning.

Inspiration

This is something so closely allied to imagination that each is dependent on the other. Stories about the courage, unselfishness or other virtues of great men and women have immense potential, as they help the Cub Scouts to think about the value of such qualities and try to emulate their heroes. Children need spiritual opportunity just as much as all other forms of development.

Discipline

Self-control or restraint, if you object to an unpopular word. This should be an inherent part of the games and all other activities. Most boys have an instinctive respect for the rules in sport, accepting that there would be no sport without them. To 'let off steam' is an absolute necessity for a boy's fast-build-up compression, but unless the switch operates both ways and somebody is capable of shutting off steam, the whole system runs down and so does Akela's. Even a few moments of physical restraint and mental concentration in one evening are vitally important parts of training.

Fun

This creeps into all our categories and lists, and quite right too, for it is of prime importance. But it does not mean one long succession of hilarious games. It should be inherent in everything: it should be fun simply to belong, fun to find out and to try, fun to do and to achieve, even fun to fail and to have to try again. Remember, too, that a really successful programme should be fun for everybody—even the Cub Scout leaders!

Who is going to do the job?

The Cub Scout leaders should form a team who share the responsibility for both planning the programme and for carrying it out. Akela, as the leader of the team, should see to it that all have equal opportunity; also that everybody takes every chance to train and to practise new skills. It is obviously an advantage if some members of the team have special aptitudes or are prepared to specialise, but this should not be to the detriment of their all-round contribution. No-one should monopolise any one subject, otherwise nobody else ever gets a look-in and, if the expert is temporarily out of action, the activity comes to an abrupt halt.

Akela should know each one well enough to be able to assess their potential capabilities as well as their limitations. They should not be asked to give more time than they can afford, considering any prior claims like family or job. For this reason it is not possible to make any firm suggestions about when or how often the Pack Scouters should meet. But meet they must, to discuss and to plan; and, within reason, the more often the better. Perhaps they will only be able to get together at the end of the Pack Meeting, but this may be in danger of becoming little more than a post mortem. It is much better, if possible, to meet on a separate occasion—and if it is a regular occasion it is more likely that everybody will keep the date, especially if they know that it is really an important and productive meeting. The ideal, perhaps, is to meet in one of the leader's home, with time to relax and concentrate, and of course if a cup of tea happens to be going it is all to the good.

Akela will generally be the architect of the plan, but it should be tentative and by no means cut and dried. Suggestions and constructive criticism should be encouraged from everybody, so that the whole team feel that they are sharing the responsibility, first for long-term planning and then the short-term details without confusing the two. Akela should set the sights, taking the long-term view of the year or the season ahead, keeping over-all aims in mind and looking for themes, targets and projects, before getting down to details and individual problems.

Responsibility for various parts of the programme will usually be allocated to those who volunteer, though some tactful persuasion may be necessary at times! Akela must have complete faith in the team, and once a job has been allocated, an Assistant Cub Scout Leader should be allowed to get on with it, knowing that help and advice is there if required.

Frequently, different people will approach an activity in a different way, and this should be encouraged, for there is no one right way of doing most things and variety in approach will add to the interest for the Pack.

If things go wrong, and they do for all of us at times, Akela should feel free to discuss the point with the individual, helping to evaluate the problem, and work out improvements for next time.

As a general principle sharing leadership means effective consultation in the planning and equally effective co-operation in the action.

The jobs need not be limited to the Warranted Scouters. If you are lucky enough to have Instructors, they may not wish to be involved with the long-term planning, but they should be kept busy with their special skills and with a variety of activities, and they should at least know why they are doing it and how it fits in with the general plan. Cub Scout Instructors bring with them the vitality and enthusiasm of teenagers, possibly specialised knowledge from their own experience as Venture Scouts or Ranger Guides and they can be of immense value in the forward-look of the Pack.

The Scout Leader, Assistants and Patrol Leaders should be invited to give occasional help, particularly with the older boys, though it should always be remembered that they have their own priorities.

In addition to these sources of help, a parent or friend can often be found to undertake a certain subject for a limited period. Akela should carefully brief helpers beforehand to ensure that the sessions are short enough and the subject matter suitable for Cubs. Specialists are prone to lose their sense of proportion! Some, of a more delicate constitution, may not feel able to face the hurly-burly of a Pack Meeting, but would be willing to take a few boys at a time in their own homes to demonstrate their own hobby. On such occasions Cubs are usually excellent ambassadors, being temporarily intimidated, and many a regular helper has been captured by one Cub's infectious grin. Cub Scout Leaders who complain that they can never get any help from anybody usually have themselves to blame, having never asked anybody, or perhaps not asked in the right way.

This lay help is particularly important for the leader who is short-handed, who may have been skimming through the foregoing paragraphs, green with envy or maybe pink with indignation at the assumption that there is a large team of Assistants.

In rural areas particularly help of any sort may be extremely hard to find, but nobody should be content to remain short-handed, however small the Pack. To become a 'one-man band' is against the rules and constitutes a real danger: it deters others from offering their help and future continuity is endangered. If such a crisis occurs and you find yourself left on your own, it may be better to give the Cub Scouts a holiday for a couple of weeks and use those two Pack nights to make an all out effort to find help. Otherwise the boys will be denied real Cub Scouting and have to make do with the restricted programme which at the best is all one person can manage to give. In searching for help it is a mistake to assume 'He would never do it', or 'She is much too busy . . .' They are the very people who might respond to B.-P.'s slogan: 'Softly, softly catchee monkey'. So through the Scouters of the Troop, the Group Council, the Parish Magazine and other Organisations, help should constantly be sought; though probably the best hope lies in the personal approach to parents or friends, who may be enticed into the trap with quite a small piece of monkey-nut.

And finally the most obvious and most important source of help: the Group Scout Leader. He is as much concerned with the Pack as with any other section, and he should be consulted and involved with all stages of planning.

When to Plan?

Ideally programmes should be planned in advance for each year, season, month, week. This may sound a bit too much of an ordeal, but experience shows that it is necessary if we are really going to accomplish our aims.

Yearly Programme

This is little more than a skeleton on which the whole body will slowly be built, and a large sheet of paper is necessary for the purpose. The fixed events of the year are usually known in advance, such as St. George's Day, Scout Job Week, and national events, not forgetting local support for national targets such as Conservation projects or Accident Prevention Weeks. Then come County, District, Parish or Group events, which may be culled from newsletters or bulletins, or from the

Group Scout Leader, who should be involved with all stages of planning. Some of these things may call for preparation, maybe weeks ahead, like the Pack Holiday or a handcraft exhibition or District Sports. Unless such things are planned in advance the Pack may become known as the lot who never join in anything or are never properly prepared.

Seasonal Programme

In order to break down the programme for the year and make it easier to handle, it is advisable to divide it into three parts, based on the three school terms. The Pack's activities must be governed to some extent by the time of year, and each season offers its own special opportunities, as well as its own drawbacks to be taken into consideration.

Tackling the four months immediately ahead, we find the Annual fixtures already blocked in, and to these can be added the crop of current events. For instance: starting in September, after the school holidays, we have the last chances to plan outdoor activities, expeditions, study of trees in autumn, migratory birds or other interests which have developed during the summer. The 'fixtures' of Guy Fawkes night, Halloween and Christmas suggest the necessary planning for parties, special handcrafts, acting and singing, as well as the Christmas Good Turn.

Each season in turn will suggest its own special activities and interests. If these can be planned on the wide basis of four months in advance, it will help to keep the Pack on its right course when we get down to the more detailed monthly programme that follows.

It is at this stage that copies should be issued to each Cub Scouter, to remind them of any tasks that they have already undertaken, and also to encourage their own ideas so that they may come up with all sorts of bright suggestions for development in detail.

Monthly Programme

What a relief it is for the Cub Scout leader team, when they sit down to consider the four weeks immediately ahead, to find the main events already blocked in. Not that County or District dates should be allowed to jostle the Pack's own plans and individual considerations out of the picture. They should help one, rather, to establish fresh objectives, sometimes to choose a 'theme' for a month, or special projects which will need more than one meeting to develop. The main activity or focal point for each evening could be planned at this juncture, though, as always with Cub Scout activities, they must be open to adaptation when one gets down to details.

Weekly Programme

This, of course, is the most important one of all. Although Pack Holidays, expeditions, Group shows and County rallies are exciting highlights in the year, the real business of Cub Scouting takes place week by week at ordinary Pack Meetings. It is then that the boy will learn about Scouting, enjoy the fun and, however unknowingly, absorb some of its values. It is then that the leaders get their best opportunity to achieve the aims of Scouting.

Therefore, having cleared the decks, as it were, with due attention to the wide planning of Yearly, Seasonal and Monthly programmes, we are going to spend very much more time and attention on planning the weekly programme in detail.

How and when you get down to the detailed planning must be entirely up to you. Perhaps you will do most of it at the monthly planning meeting, or perhaps there will be time at the end of one Pack Meeting to finalise the bits and pieces for the next. At some moment it must be done and written down for each leader and instructor, roughly timing the events and deciding definitely who is going to do what, and the gear or equipment for which they will each be responsible. As a team, of course, all scouters will help each other, if only to the extent of keeping law and order, and giving an example to the Cubs by listening, rather than indulging in adult chatter among themselves.

Some Packs seem to have the same type of programme every week, and everyone knows just what to expect: the same old games, the same dog-eared charts and books, the same leaders instructing in the same tests; in fact the only real achievement of the evening seems to be to teach Cub Scouts how to suffer boredom without complaint!

The following is typical of the shape and timing of what might be called 'a traditional' programme:

5 mins.	Opening Ceremony: Grand Howl, Flag Break, Inspection, Subs.
10 mins.	Game: to let off steam.
20 mins.	Work: some form of badge-work, new or revisionary.
5 mins.	Quieter game: to practise the skill.
15 mins.	Interest activity of a different sort.
10 mins.	Game: to put it into practice.
20 mins.	Focal point: Making something, acting, a yarn or surprise item.

5 mins. Closing Ceremony: Grand Howl, Flag, Prayers.

—

90 mins.

But, although this is a sound foundation on which to build, it is a good thing to get right away from that set format occasionally, so that the Cubs will have no idea what is going to happen at any given moment.

Practical suggestions in detail for the above 'traditional' programme and for several others of contrasting types, will be found in Part 2.

Where does the Pack meet?

The environment in which your Pack meets may largely influence your choice of programme and, indeed, the people who are taking part in it. It is obvious that everything we suggest cannot suit everybody, but most activities can be adapted in some way and you should be slow to abandon an idea just because of environmental difficulties. There is still an 'out' in an urban area, though it may be a park, a playing field, school yard or even the street, though this would call for more careful planning and better control.

There are many rural Packs who don't use their outdoor opportunities as much as they might, and would often be glad to swap for the more concentrated facilities of a town. But there are still plenty of activities which can be enjoyed by all these different types of Packs, and this is where your own imagination may be challenged.

In this book we will try to suggest practical alternatives for urban or rural Packs, as indeed for wet weather or fine, but there is still plenty of room for adaptation and for you to use your own environment to your own advantage.

What equipment will be needed?

Several questions arise:

What gear do we need?

Have we got it?

Can we improvise?

Can we make it, borrow it, buy it?

Improvisation and imagination can do wonders, but not if it comes to using chewed bits of string for knotting, instead of proper cord or rope. Borrowing from the Troop may solve many difficulties, but unless the gear is kept and returned in good condition, the Scout Leader may understandably become a little dubious about lending it the next time.

The Pack should possess the necessary equipment to put over the Arrow Training scheme in an imaginative way, which means an assortment of training aids and plenty of materials for the Cubs to use. There should be enough games equipment to allow for plenty of variety, and the imaginative Scouter team will constantly be adding to it. Funds for necessities should be forthcoming, by applying to the Group Council via a sympathetic Group Scout Leader who will explain just why it is necessary for the Pack to have two footballs, six packets of plasticene and an old pram, if anybody happens to have one. Other short-term items may often be borrowed for special occasions, perhaps from the District or other Packs. The Local Education Authority will be able to lend or hire more expensive equipment for occasional use, such as projectors or tape recorders. But the boys' own families and friends will probably prove to be the best source of supply for the odds and ends which an active Pack needs. It is surprising how often the Pack can make good use of what other people term 'junk'.

Suggested list of Pack Equipment

Cupboard or box to contain equipment, preferably with several sections.
Notice board.

Make and Do Equipment

Scissors
Cotton, needles, pins
Plasticine
Rubber bands
Drawing pins
Cardboard
Adhesive tape
Paper clips
Pencils, crayons, chalk
Coloured felt tip pens
Paints, brushes
Scrap paper
Plaster of paris
Transparent adhesive sheeting
Heel ball
Cotton reels
Match boxes
Glue
Balsa wood
Polythene
Polystyrene
Polystyrene cutters
Tool box

Games box

Large ball, small ball
Bean bags
Empty plastic bottles
Gym mat
Dice and shaker
Rope
Cricket bat
Hoops

Dressing-up box

Skirts — slashed up the middle make cloaks for knights or highwaymen

A bright strip of satin makes a pirate's sash
A coloured square — a robber's face mask or a cowboy's neckerchief
An old sheet can dress a sheik or a ghost
Dish cloths sprayed with silver paint make chain-mail
Egg boxes fashioned become armour
Crowns with jewels, masks and space helmets can be made from papier-mâché
Discarded hats, broken swords and dusty clothes from the last jumble sale

Training aids and charts

SCOUTING magazine publishes a large range of useful charts

Flannelgraph board	Practice telephone and telephone directory
Pictures of the jungle animals	24-hour clock
Proper First Aid kit	Timetables
First Aid practice kit	Union Flag
Street map of the area	Coloured ropes for knotting
Model of local area	Compass (magnetic)
Brushes and soap	Fire-lighting demonstration model
Shoe cleaning equipment	Simple science equipment
Tea pot and tea making equipment	Conjuring set

Books

Songs	Stories
Local history	Games
Junior science	Puppetry
Nature	Play acting
Handcrafts	Prayers

What else?

Some very important aspects of planning which must not be overlooked:

Parents

There are those who are interested and want to know what is going on, others who don't seem to care, so long as their boy is out from under their feet. But all must be treated with the consideration they deserve. They have the right to be told of our plans and should not be left to the somewhat garbled accounts their sons may give them, or even the written notes which their sons may forget to give them. The more we look for co-operation from all, the more we are likely to get help from some, often from unexpected quarters. Most parents will co-operate if asked specifically to help with such things as Jumble Sales, making costumes or cups of tea; whereas general invitations make people cautious. They fear they may be letting themselves in for more than they bargained for. Some might be willing to provide transport, give First Aid instruction or test for a Book Reader badge; and many Dads, might be agreeably intrigued with the requirements of the Fisherman or Scientist badges. It is a wise Akela who can assess the skills of the parents as well as those of the sons. Too often too many parents don't know enough about Cub Scouting and the opportunities it offers for outside help. Leaders should visit parents in their own homes, which will establish a more personal relationship, leading to mutual understanding and assistance.

An occasional Parent's Evening or Social is of tremendous value, especially before an event like a Pack Holiday, which calls for forms to be signed and expenses to be met. They should know that the money is going to be put to good account for the benefit of their boys. They should be given the opportunity to get to know the people who are undertaking these responsibilities. Often they are astounded by the way in which their unruly youngsters respond to the influences of this remarkable person known as Akela. Joint evenings with the Troop will encourage parents to take a long-term view and a better understanding of the world aspect of the Movement.

Sixers' Councils

Sixers can help at the Pack Meeting by organising their Sixes when necessary, but they also can help the Pack Scouters through the Sixers' Council. This is rather a special but informal meeting and if it can be held at Akela's home it is the best background. Here the boys' own ideas can be put forward, suggesting a Pack good turn, or perhaps a place for the next Pack expedition. Projects can be discussed and decisions made about them: whether to spend money on a new football, or wood for a puppet theatre, how to help the shy boy in the Pack to feel part of the Group. New games can be tried out and plans made to include the Cub in a wheelchair.

The Sixers will help you to keep a finger on the 'pulse' of the Pack, and if you listen to them you will hear many snippets of information which will help you to understand why certain boys are behaving in certain ways. Perhaps there is a new baby in the family, or a pet has died, or a chance to play in the school football team is causing Scouting to take a back seat for a while.

Public Relations

This is a job that is usually undertaken by the Group Scout Leader or a Group Public Relations Officer, but he should be kept informed of Pack activities, past, present and future; not only for the benefit of parents but of the Group Council and friends of Scouting: school teachers, ministers, the Parish magazines and local press. We must learn to blow our own trumpets in a modest way, but never to give the impression that we are a closed shop, or run by such peculiar people that the general public feel we are best left alone.

PART 2
Programmes

A programme based on the 'traditional' time-table

5mins. **Opening Ceremonies** Grand Howl, Flagbreak, Inspection, Subs.

10 mins. **Games** *Skittles*

Purpose: fun and alertness.

Chalk a triangle on the floor in the middle of the room, and stand a washing-up liquid bottle in each of the three corners. One boy in the centre has to keep all three 'skittles' upright. The Pack forms a circle round him, and are armed with three or four tennis balls, with which they try to knock down the skittles. If they succeed in knocking them all down at once the one who threw the last ball changes places with the boy in the triangle.

20 mins. **Arrow Work**

New boys. Cut out and colour a jungle animal from a polystyrene tile, using a polystyrene cutter (available from 'Do-it-Yourself' shops) and a previously prepared cardboard template.

Physical Skills (Bronze Arrow). Ball throwing, forward roll, and leap frog: (trying to improve on own performance during the evening).

Commnications (Silver Arrow). In pairs using a tape recorder if possible, practice making and answering a telephone call. Criticise one another. When all are confident, go with an Assistant Cub Scout Leader to a telephone box and make calls to a pre-arranged recipient.

More Knotting (Gold Arrow). Knotting practice in pairs, take it in turns to rescue and be rescued using the bowline. Practice hanking a long rope.

5 mins. **Game** *Floating feathers*

Purpose: fun and team spirit.

Cubs sit in two teams facing one another, either on the floor or on chairs, but not hard up against the walls. Several feathers are thrown into the air between them, and each team must try to blow the feathers over the heads of their opponents. If it is a season of heavy colds, use home-made fans made of newspaper.

20 mins. **Potato puppets**

Purpose: finger skill and imagination.

The previous week everybody is asked to bring a large, scrubbed potato. (Given the average memory of a Cub, the leader should have several extra ones in reserve.) Using a vegetable corer, a hole should be cut half way into the potato, large enough to take the index or second finger. Construct a face, using felt-tipped pens, or by sticking on pieces of paper, wool or silver foil. By punching a hole through the middle of a piece of paper with a finger, one can make an effective poncho to be worn under the potato head. When everyone has finished ask your Sixers to form a Panel of Judges to award small prizes for the funniest, the weirdest or the most recognisable. Potato puppets do not last very long, so it is not worth while spending too much time on them.

15 mins. **Six Jolly Workmen**

Purpose: Observation, teamwork and fun.

Each Six decides privately among themselves on an occupation or profession which they are going to mime; encourage them to choose less obvious jobs such as a school-crossing patrol-man, a pneumatic drill operator, check-out cashier in a supermarket, ambulance driver, fireman, milkman. Taking turns to perform their mime to the rest of the Pack, each Six begins by chanting: 'We are six jolly workmen', to which the other Cubs reply: 'What can you do?' The Six respond: 'We'll show you!' and proceed with their mime, in which all should take part, some contributing background or crowd effects, although in complete silence. This should go on until the rest of the Pack guess the occupation presented.

10 mins. **Sing-Song** A few songs which everyone can enjoy even if they do not know all the words yet.

5 mins. **Closing Ceremonies** Grand Howl; Flagdown; Prayers; for all people who work in our town (including some of those recently mimed).

Equipment needed:

Chalk, 3 washing-up liquid bottles, tennis balls
Polystyrene tiles, cutter, cardboard templates of jungle animals
Mat (for forward roll)
Tape recorder, money for telephone calls
Small knotting ropes, long rope for hanking
A dozen or so feathers
Large scrubbed potatoes, vegetable corers, felt-tipped pens, scraps of material, wool, paper; pins or glue, small prizes
List of songs
Suitable prayers

A programme for out-of-doors

We all know the importance of the 'out' in Scouting, but it is not always appreciated that this should begin in the Pack.

If you live in the country you may be able to arrange to meet at a suitable starting place. Town Packs may have to organise parents to help with transport to the nearest park or further afield. This need not be limited to high summer. After the summer holidays particularly, before boys have adjusted to being shut in school all day, they will appreciate any efforts to take them out into some open space.

Remember most activities take longer to do out-of-doors and try to avoid playing the same games that you can play indoors; use the space to full advantage.

The Grand Howl may take place before setting out, and be followed with a timely reminder concerning litter, road safety, or the Country Code as may be necessary.

20 mins. **Game** *Non-stop rounders*

Purpose: to let off steam and keep fit.

(One of the versions of rounders played 10 minutes each way)

The players are set as for ordinary rounders, but behind the batting base is a large tea-chest or cardboard packing case. Play begins and the bowler continues to bowl whenever the ball is returned to him, whether or not there is a batsman at the base. A batsman is out if he is bowled or caught, or if he fails to get into position before the bowler bowls the ball.

30 mins. **Tree profile**

Each Six chooses a different tree and makes a chart of it—including a drawing of the tree and one of its fruits, and bark and leaf rubbings if in season. They can be shown how to estimate the height of the tree, measure its girth, work out a bird's-eye view of its shape, discuss what the wood is used for.

Alternatively, younger boys can work on this project, whilst older boys with an adult collect fungi or fruits, or go pond-dipping. They might also produce a poster to warn the younger ones of the 'dangers of the countryside'.

Some boys may prefer to arrange a collection of autumn leaves on a postcard and cover them with transparent adhesive sheeting to take back home.

15 mins. **Wide Game** *Take-off*

Purpose: fun, stalking practice if the area is wooded, otherwise physical activity.

The area of play must be clearly defined. Each Six is given an assortment of articles (the same for each Six), e.g. nut, bolt, nail, string, rubber band, paper clip. A piece of wool is tied round each boy's arm. The 'astronaut' (one of the leaders) sits in the centre of the area, with a separate tin for each Six. The Cub Scouts must try and deliver all the parts of the new space rocket, which is still on the secret list, without being spotted by other designers who are wanting to copy their ideas. The 'other designers' are the Assistants who roam about the area, and try to break the wool on the boys' arms. If they are successful then the Cub can continue to the astronaut but must declare that the part he is carrying is faulty, and must correctly answer a general knowledge question before his part becomes useful again.

The first Six to get all parts into their tin are the winners, and perhaps a firework rocket could be released by the astronaut, a whistle signals the end of the game, when all must come to the centre.

10 mins. **Country Alphabet**

Purpose: to quieten boys down before setting off for home; nature study.

Cubs sit in Sixes. The leader calls a letter of the alphabet and each Six must name some visible natural object beginning with that letter. They must avoid repeating anything already said.

Closing Prayers—thanksgiving for the countryside, or for some particular aspect of nature.

Equipment needed:

Small ball, rounders bat (if wished), cardboard packing case or something suitable as a back stop

Large and small sheets of paper for each Six

Heel ball, shoe polish pad, garden cane, tape measure

Compass, felt-tipped pens

Polythene bags or other pond-dipping equipment: nets, jam jars, etc. postcards, transparent adhesive sheeting
Bag of odd objects for each Six, wool for tying round arms, list of questions, firework rocket and/or whistle
Suitable prayers

A programme using bases

The next type of programme is a particularly good one to use if you have some new helpers coming along. They will play a real part in the meeting by looking after one of the bases, and not just stand on the edge of things all the evening. They can be carefully briefed for their own job, and as they carry out the same project three times, as the various groups move around, they have a chance of being highly successful with the last group which will give increased confidence, even if the first try was not so good.
Depending on numbers, you may need to increase the number of bases. Preferably Akela should be free to keep an eye on everything.

5 mins. **Opening Ceremonies** Grand Howl; Flagbreak, Inspection, Subs.

10 mins. **Game** *World Travel*

Purpose: to keep everyone alert and involved. All Cub Scouts and leaders sit in a circle and each choses the name of a country. One person in the centre is the aeroplane and announces that he is flying from, say, 'Japan to Canada'. The two people with those names have to try and exchange places while the aeroplane will try and get into one of their seats before them. If he does, the player caught out becomes the aeroplane, and the ex-aeroplane takes the name of the country.

60 mins. **Bases** Divide the Pack into groups to work around the bases in a clockwise direction spending 20 minutes at each base. Adjust groups and bases according to the number in your Pack. Bases might include some of the tests from the Home Help badge: cleaning silver or brasswork, ironing a scarf, poaching an egg, or these three we have selected.

Base 1 Cooking sausages Each Cub fries two sausages. Provide bread rolls so that they can be eaten 'hot-dog' style. If your headquarters hasn't a cooker, borrow camping gas stoves.

Base 2 Making a hot drink Discuss how to make tea, coffee and cocoa. Then the group makes all three between them, and all taste them to determine their success. Some may like to try lemon tea too. All utensils and crockery are washed-up and the best methods of doing this are discussed.

Base 3 Clothes folding and shoe cleaning Demonstration of how to fold a shirt or jacket and a pair of shorts ready for packing. All practise on

some 'spares' brought for the occasion. Discussion and demonstration of shoe cleaning. Everyone cleans their own shoes, or the Cubs should be asked the week before to bring a pair of Dad's shoes to clean as a good turn. Have plenty of equipment and protective covering for both Cubs and the floor.

10 mins. **Game** *Packing the case*

Purpose: action, and reinforcement of learning. A washing line is fixed across one end of the room. Sixes in relay formation stand at the other end. Pegged on the line for each Six are an old shirt, a pair of shorts and a pair of socks. In front of each Six is a shopping bag or small case. On the signal the Sixer picks up the bag, runs to unpeg the washing and folds it as he has been shown earlier in the meeting, before packing it into the bag. Then he runs back down the hall and around his own Six and back to the washing line, takes out the clothes, pegs them on the line and runs to the back of his Six, handing the bag to the second boy in the line as he passes.

5 mins. **Closing Ceremonies** Grand Howl; Flagdown; Prayers;—for Mums—for help to remember to do a good turn every day of the coming week.

Equipment needed:

Cooker, frying pans, plates, forks
Sausages, fat for frying, bread rolls
Tea, coffee, cocoa, milk, sugar, lemon, kettle, milk saucepan
Cups or mugs, teapot, jugs, dish-cloths, washing-up liquid, tea towels
Jacket, shirt, trousers
Shoe cleaning equipment, protective covering for floor
Washing line, clothes pegs, old shirts, pairs of shorts, pairs of socks, shopping bags or small cases
Suitable prayers

A programme based on a theme

The programmes so far have been a hotchpotch of ideas. In the second one the out-of-doors dictated the type of activity, in the third the method of using bases gave a certain structure to the programme. It will often be found helpful to have a theme running through the meeting, providing a continuous focus for thought. Let's suppose we have chosen 'Safety' as the theme. The Cub Scouts at all stages of Arrow work would be helped to see how the various skills are of use to them in real life. The boy learning to make a bowline would not be doing so just to get a tick in his book, but would see it as a safety measure used by rock-climbers and steeplejacks, and everyone can join in the fun if it is included in a game where the Six have to be rescued. The water safety rules could be developed into a play-acting project for the whole Pack. Everyone enjoys the acting, and will learn about the water safety rules. Each Six could produce a poster about 'Hazards in the Home', drawing pictures or cutting them out from a mail-order catalogue and sticking them on a sheet of paper: a baby in a nightdress near a fire, a pan handle protruding over the edge of a cooker or other hazards. The following week the boys should be able to tell you some of the causes of accidents in the home.

For the leaders, a theme is a help in planning. It is possible to spark off ideas more easily when everyone has the same theme in mind. As described above, it also helps the meeting to be planned 'across the board' with everyone joining in all activities, rather than always dividing the Pack up into Bronze, Silver and Gold Arrow working groups. Sometimes an activity will be a repeat for the older boys, but it can often be given a slightly different slant, or they can help the leaders run the activity, and anyway a little revision is not a bad thing from time to time. There is no harm in an eight year old hearing something about activities at present beyond his capabilities. Although the broader aspects of a subject might be beyond his understanding some of the basic safety rules, perhaps water safety, may sink in. For after all, the important thing is that the boy should behave sensibly from an early age — it is never too soon for him to learn to take care of himself.

This method can often give a more even distribution of work for the leaders. It is also useful if there are not enough leaders to take all the many sub-groups of each Arrow activity area, which sometimes have to be handled all at the same time.

Not every activity needs to fit in with the theme; a completely different 'surprise' item may be included, to give an extra 'zing' to the programme.

A theme such as 'Safety' can be developed in so many ways that it could be useful as a general theme for a month; home safety, road safety, water safety and the Country Code could all be included.

A programme based on the theme Policemen

We began thinking about seasonal planning with the autumn season. If we now take one month from that season—September—and look at the calendar, we see that September 29th is the day dedicated to St. Michael the Archangel. Just as St. George is the patron saint of Scouts, St. Michael is the patron saint of policemen. So, this could give us an idea for an autumn meeting theme for the last week in September.

It will make a greater impact on the boys and be much more fun if you can persuade a policeman to come along to the Pack Meeting. Most of them are only too willing to help. Ask your policeman well in advance of the date you require him and give a thorough briefing so that he may know exactly what is required of him.

10 mins. **Opening Ceremonies** Grand Howl, Flagbreak, Inspection.

As well as the normal inspection, this week there is a sort of inspection of knowledge, each Cub being asked a question such as: 'What number would you dial in an emergency?', 'Where is the nearest police station?', 'What would you do if fire broke out here and now?', 'What is the Green Cross Code?', 'Which is the right way to use a Zebra crossing?', 'What would you do if you saw someone acting suspiciously?'.

10 mins. **Game** *'Stop Thief!'*

Purpose: alertness.

A circle game which includes everyone.

The game 'Snatch the Cap' is adapted to fit in with the theme. The Cubs stand in a circle with an old cap in the middle. One boy is the snatcher and runs round the outside of the circle, choosing one boy to tap on the back as he passes. He then races into the circle, through the gap that he has left. He must snatch up the cap and get back to his place without being caught by the boy he has tapped. The two boys must play 'cat and mouse' for a while, the first boy (the snatcher) making a few false moves and feints before finally snatching up the cap, for he cannot be 'caught' until he has it in his hand. If he is caught then, he rejoins the circle and the other boy becomes the snatcher.

Or, an alternative game is:

'Stop, Wait, Go'

Purpose: fun, self-control, and traffic light drill.

Each Six needs a single die or small cube, two faces of which are coloured red, two amber and two green. As an alternative, three coloured cards may be used, each boy choosing one from the three cards held face down by a leader, who shuffles between draws.

The object is to get the whole Six across a busy traffic junction to the other side of the room. Each boy in turn runs half way up the room, where he stops to throw the die, or draw a card. If he gets a red, he returns to the start and another boy sets out; if it is green, he can go, and runs safely across to the other side; if it is an amber, the boy must wait where he is until another member of his Six gets a green, when they may proceed together. Any boy who goes when he shouldn't, or doesn't go when he should, becomes a road casualty, and his Six loses a life.

20 mins. **'Walkie-talkie sets'** and **'Code-breakers'**

Divide the Pack into two groups:

—the younger ones make and test string telephones (walkie-talkie sets). These are made with plastic disposable cups, with a hole pierced in the base and string threaded through and knotted on the inside. The string must be kept taut in use.. They may go on to experiment and find out if four telephones can be joined together successfully.

—the older boys experiment with various liquids to find one which makes the best invisible ink (the 'code-breakers'). Try as great a variety as possible: lemon juice, orange juice, vinegar, sugar or salt in water. An adult should supervise the heating of the papers, when finding out which message will 'develop' most clearly. A dry heat, such as the sole-plate of an iron, is better than a candle or match flame, which could set fire to the paper. (See Codes and Ciphers in Part 3).

These activities are an introduction to the Scientist badge. You may observe that some boys are particularly enthusiastic about them, and arrange to develop their interest further until they gain the badge.

5 mins. **Identification Parade**

Purpose: observation, and the self-control which is necessary for a quiet game.

Each leader and the policeman in turn go out of the room and return with one item of their uniform altered in some way. The boys are asked to spot the difference and remember it for a check later.

20 mins. **Policeman's discussion with the Pack**

Arrange with the policeman beforehand to bring something with him which will capture the attention of the Cub Scouts. Handcuffs, perhaps, or his own walkie-talkie, or even a patrol car which they can examine. He can then go on to discuss with them what they can do to help the police. For example, what to do when leaving a house unoccupied and why these things are done; or the reasons for the rules in the Highway Code, both for pedestrians and cyclists.

15 mins. **Game** *'Identikits'*

Purpose: observation, concentration and fun. A large photograph of the face of a well-known person is required for each Six. Suitable ones can be found in television magazines. These are prepared by being stuck on card and cut up into five pieces. The pieces are hidden in different parts of the room before the meeting begins, and the leader prepares a set of five clues for each Six: 'Under the piano', 'under the mat', 'behind the door' or, perhaps, indicating their location by compass directions. If these clues are written in a simple code, it will make the game that much more intriguing.

The Pack is told that some 'wanted' men are believed to be hiding in the room, and that each Six is being asked by the police to find one of them. The clues are given to the Sixers, and a 'key' if the code needs deciphering, and the hunt is on. If several pieces of different photographs are hidden in the same place, they may need to be numbered or coloured on the back, so that the Sixes can identify their own piece.

10 mins. **Yarn**

Two Cubs were playing football on the way to school one morning, and they suddenly realised that they were late and would get into trouble. There was only one thing to do—take a short-cut across a railway siding. But they knew that this was trespassing, and also dangerous. Trevor said he was going to risk it, and that he couldn't face the angry Mr. Pilkington if he was late. Howard decided to go the long way round, preferring Mr. Pilkington's anger to his Dad's if he found out that he had gone across the railway siding after being told not to. Trevor arrived in good time, but while Howard was running as fast as he could, a car pulled up beside him, and a man jumped out and accused him of stealing a clock from his shop. Howard quickly denied this and began to explain that he was running because he was late for school and, anyway, he would have had nowhere to hide a clock as he was wearing only a T shirt and shorts. He recognised the man as the Venture Scout Leader he had seen at the Group Headquarters on Friday. The Venture Scout Leader apologised for not recognising Howard and for making such a silly mistake in thinking that he had stolen the clock. Then suddenly Howard remembered that, as he was passing the shop, he had seen a red-haired young man putting something into a bag and jumping into a Volkswagen 'Beetle' car. He had particularly noticed a Donald Duck transfer on the lid of the boot. The Venture Scout Leader thanked Howard and, to make up for delaying him offered him a lift to school, which was right opposite the Police Station where he was going to report the theft. Howard arrived at school just as the bell was ringing. Asked by the astonished Trevor how he had made it so fast, Howard replied that it was not so much a matter of fast legs as of sharp eyes.

5 mins. **Closing Ceremonies:** Grand Howl, Flagdown, Prayers—for all policemen: detectives, crime prevention officers, accident prevention officers, the policeman on the local beat; for help to be observant, so that we can help others, and can observe when a good turn needs doing.

Equipment needed:

Policeman! Ready briefed
Questions for Inspection
Old cap
Copy of the Highway Code
Plastic, disposable cups, string, scissors
Several small jars containing liquids for testing as invisible inks, iron or other means of heating paper
Jigsaw puzzles, five clues for each Six, and a key to the codes, if necessary
Suitable yarn
Suitable prayer

Special Pack Meeting

About every three months it is a good idea to have a 'surprise' evening, when the programme breaks right away from the normal pattern, and the boys get the impression that anything may happen! This is called a 'Special Pack Meeting', and is usually based on a special theme or story, which binds the whole evening together and links the activities. Some are purely for fun, some include in a different guise some of the Arrow or Proficiency Badge Skills in practical form, and there is an opportunity for more imaginative and unusual items.

The life story of B.-P. makes a good theme for such an evening, especially if it is near Founder's Day, February 22nd. Topical subjects such as a forthcoming Jamboree or Olympic Games or Cup Final can be developed into interesting programmes. Or an evening could be planned based on a book which has recently been told or read as a serial, such as *Treasure Island* or *Swallows and Amazons*.

Here is a programme based on space.

Space mission for peace

The United Nations are sending out teams of explorers to the planets, to tell any possible inhabitants they might meet there, about 'Planet Earth'. They are anxious to establish good relationships with other planets and not just trying to use their resources for our own benefit.

As the journeys will be long ones, it is necessary to use very young people, and The Scout Association has been chosen as so many of the astronauts who went to the moon had been Scouts and showed that they had qualities of self-reliance and responsibility.

To get into training each Six of the Pack will make a trial journey tonight.

First of all, each Cub Scout must take a fitness test to see if he can stand up to the hardship of the journey:

10 mins. **Game**—based on Growing up

As a Six relay race, each boy first does a forward roll,

then all leap-frog over the Second, then the Sixer stands in front of his Six and throws the ball to each one in turn.

10 mins. **Equipment making**

Equipment is important and everyone will need a space-helmet. These can be made from cardboard boxes and aluminium foil (the Cub Scouts could be asked the previous week to bring a suitable box). Each Six should have a special identification mark on their helmets so that others will know which space rocket they belong to.

5 mins. Take-off—The Sixer ties a rope to the waist of each boy using a bowline. When all are safely anchored in the 'rocket' he applies to 'control' for instructions.

5 mins. 'Set a course N.W. from your Six corner to reach the nearest planet to be visited—Mercury. Proceed 11 million miles—1 step equals 1 million miles! (Work out as appropriate for your headquarters). N.B. This first clue will be different for each Six so that they all congregate at the same point. After this they all proceed together.

5 mins. At Mercury leave behind a drawing of a British bird, a British flower and a British tree.

5 mins. Proceed South 4 million miles to Venus. Leave there a map of the area around your headquarters.

10 mins. Proceed S.E. 6 million miles to Mars. Celebrate your arrival with a 'Mars Feast'. The Cub Scouts sit in a circle and a die is thrown by each in turn. When one throws a 'six' he runs to the centre, where there is an enamel plate bearing the Mars bar and a knife and fork. Beside it is a hat, coat and scarf, which the boy must put on before he sits down to his feast, slicing the hard, sticky sweet. He continues eating until the next 'six' is thrown, when he must instantly divest himself and hand over to the next Cub.

10 mins. Each Six makes up a television commercial-type 'jingle', about any kind of food eaten on Earth, which might be worth advertising to the Martians. Each Six sings its 'jingle' to the rest of the Pack.

10 mins. Proceed due East 5 million miles to Jupiter. Here the Cub Scouts have to demonstrate one sport which is enjoyed by men on Earth. Each rocket

team does a mime for the others to guess, but a check should be made by the leaders that they have not all chosen football!

10 mins. 3 million miles to the N.E. is Saturn. Here the atmosphere is so rarified that there are few living creatures and the few natives speak no recognisable language. The rocket men leave with them a model in plasticine of an animal to be found on Earth.

Finally the crew return to Earth. Because of the problem of weightlessness all spacemen must run backwards, making three circuits of Planet Earth (headquarters), before they can make a safe landing (sitting down in their Six corner).

Space passports, previously made by the leaders, are then issued to all Cub Scouts who are eligible for consideration for the United Nations, and a special medal presented to the leader of the special space crew.

Closing prayers—for astronauts and explorers
—for statesmen, working for better understanding between all people.

(The times suggested are purely indicative and some activities may have to be deleted. Time must be allowed for Opening and Closing Ceremonies and for explanation of the development of each activity).

Equipment needed:

Gym mats, balls
Cardboard boxes, aluminium foil, felt pens
Piece of rope for each boy
Compass for each Six
Papers and pencils all round
Enamel plate, knife and fork, Mars bars, old clothes
Plasticine
Suitable prayers

A programme based on one activity

Sometimes to achieve the satisfactory completion of an activity, rather more time is needed than the usual work period in a Pack programme. Rehearsing a play for an Open Evening, for instance, or handcrafts, as in the example below.

Christmas handcrafts

The Cub Scouts are warned the week before to come in old clothes or with some protective covering for their uniforms.

Some boys make nesting boxes and bird tables under the guidance of a Scouter, or a 'carpenter' friend. (Simple diagrams are available from the Royal Society for the Protection of Birds, Sandy, Bedfordshire.) These are erected in the garden of an elderly person's home or hospital as a Christmas Good Turn.

Other Cub Scouts make Christmas decorations from polystyrene tiles. Outlines of Christmas trees, stars, reindeers, and crackers to use as templates can be found in children's painting books. A Santa Claus can be given a 3D effect by adding a separate moustache, eyebrows, red nose, etc., to the basic face. Water colour paints in bright colours will improve the finished article.

A third group could make Christmas cards to send to the various friends of the Pack—Group Scout Leader, Assistant District Commissioner, Badge Examiner, or anyone who has helped in any way on outings or holidays during the year.

'Pop-up' Christmas cards or calendars are fun to make, but be careful not to use ideas already tried at school. Simple Christmas table arrangements in small tin foil dishes, or Christmas mobiles might also be suitable for the eight year olds. Five minutes at the end of the meeting devoted to a race to find the fastest clearer up, might well save the leaders much hard work afterwards!

Prayers—for hands and the pleasure of making things.
—for some aspect of Christmas as appropriate.

Equipment needed:

If it is a handcraft evening, there must be plenty of raw material and tools, and the necessary bits and pieces, in order that all Cubs shall be able to have a go.
There should also be plenty of protective covering, both for boys and for floor or tables. And, finally, the necessary equipment for cleaning up and litter containers.

A programme for an outdoor meeting in a suburban area

Many Packs meet in suburban areas and have to make the best of it. Although expeditions into the country can be arranged from time to time, this is not enough to satisfy the boys' instinct to get out and their natural desire to enjoy some Cubbing activities out-of-doors. This means that leaders should plan the best use that can be made of the immediate surroundings. Much will depend upon the particular area in which the Pack meets, but in the programme which follows some of the ideas might prove to be suitable for your Pack or easily adapted to your neighbourhood.

10 mins. **Opening Ceremonies** Grand Howl, Flagbreak, Inspection. As the Pack is going outside this evening, in the public view, the Sixers might help the leaders to ensure that Inspection is very thorough. If anoraks are to be worn, these too should be inspected, to ensure that they are as tidy as possible.

5 mins. **Briefing for 'Mission'**
Each Six is given an envelope containing details of the route to be followed, a sketch map of the area, a compass, paper and pencils, a list of things to do on the way and a second envelope containing 'sealed orders'.
An hour will probably be quite long enough for the Sixes to be out on their Mission; the subjects being carefully chosen and the Sixers well briefed. They should study their briefing before they set out, and be given a chance to ask the inevitable questions. If possible it would be wise to have an adult keeping an eye on each Six.

60 mins. **Mission** The instructions to the Sixer must be very

clearly written and might be on the following lines:

1) Turn RIGHT outside headquarters. Go NORTH till you see the Church clock. WRITE DOWN THE TIME using the 24-hour clock.
2) Turn EAST and go to the MAIN ROAD. Write down the MAKE of the first FOUR PARKED CARS you see.
3) How many LITTER BINS have you noticed between here and headquarters? Are they at the places where most litter is thrown down? If you could put up two new ones, where would you site them? MARK the places on your MAP.
4) Look in the window of the SUPERMARKET and write down the names of four things on display, the initial letter of which spell 'P A C K'.
5) Sixer, when you have done this open your 'SEALED ORDERS' but *do not* show the others. MEMORISE the message, then put the paper in the litter bin on the corner, and whisper the message to your Second. Ask him to pass on the message to the next boy in the Six and so on until the last boy in the Six is given the message. He must tell it to Akela when you return to headquarters.

   The message must only be said once and not repeated.

   (The message could be something like 'Look out for white saloon car, number ULH 552M).
6) If the Pack were to give a bench for the elderly as a Good Turn, where would be the best place to put it? A quiet place, a busy place, a grassy place? Mark your your choice on the map.
7) If you were to POST A LETTER in the postbox on the corner now, would it be collected today?
8) Now turn WEST at the end of the Car Park. It has been reported that two people have been seen acting very strangely along this road. Return to headquarters without them

seeing you, but if you can, get a full description of them. (Two leaders wearing anything which is fairly easy for the Cubs to describe: a football scarf, battered hat, carrying umbrella etc. Perhaps the Group Scout Leader and Scout Leader would help, by being the two strangers.)

5 mins. **De-Briefing** Back at headquarters the descriptions of the strange men are given and later checked when they come in to be identified. The various information collected is checked, and the whole Pack discuss the best place to fit additional litter bins, and a seat for the elderly.

5 mins. **A yarn** or a few songs might be advisable to quieten the Pack down before going home.

5 mins. **Closing Ceremonies** Grand Howl, Flagdown, Prayers—for those who work in the community: the dustbin men who clear away the litter, those who look after the elderly, those who serve in the local shops.

PART 3
Activities

Under each Activity some books are recommended as Training Aids. These are marked as follows:

* meaning that they are available from Scout Shops Ltd.

† meaning that they cost more than 50p.

The standard books for all Cub Scout activities are:

* *The Cub Scout Programme Booklet* an informative booklet written for Cubs themselves containing full details of the Cub Scout Badge, the Arrow Scheme and all the Proficiency Badges.

*†	*The Cub Scout Leader's Handbook*	written for leaders
†	*Cub Scout Games*	
†	*Activities for Cub Scout* and *Resource material for Cub Scout Proficiency Badges* (available from the Resource Centre, Gilwell Park)	

Athletics—Feats of Skill

Training aids

Books

† *Activities for Cub Scouts* (Gilwell Park)

Who might help

Teachers of physical education at local schools
Members of local amateur athletics clubs
Venture Scouts
Scouters

Planning

All the activities, from simple feats of skill to the requirements of the Athlete badge, are designed to encourage the physical development of growing boys. It is the responsibility of the leader to ensure that they are carried out with proper regard to safety rules. Any equipment used such as vaulting fences or balancing beams, should be checked before use and boys should be supervised when using them.

Ball throwing and other simple physical activities are easy to incorporate in most Pack programmes. There is rarely any difficulty in persuading boys to climb trees, an adventurous activity with maximum appeal to boys of Cub Scout age, but vaulting and high jump may require the help of a specialist. Care should be taken that a) any instructions given are by the correct methods as a boy can easily overstrain himself; b) that the right apparatus is used, such as a thick mat for forward roll, to prevent any possible damage to a boy's back, and c) that sensible light loose clothing is worn with soft shoes. Obviously standards of achievement will vary and whilst everyone should be encouraged to take part, they will not all be keen to go on to Athlete badge standard. Less athletic types can be encouraged to act as markers or recorders.

Some competition acts as a spur to further achievement, but don't let the competitive spirit override everything else. It may be better for a boy to try to improve on his own record, keeping a chart over a period of a month.

Putting it over

Some ideas for inclusion in indoor Pack Meetings to develop co-ordination:

Backward Toss Cubs lie flat on their backs and try to throw a beanbag through a hoop held upright at floor level 2 metres away.

Throwing through the legs Cubs throw a beanbag backwards between their legs, through a hoop held by the Sixer, 2 metres behind them.

Steady Hands Race Boys, carrying a plastic beaker three quarters full of water in one hand and a lighted candle in the other, run round the course. If a contestant spills any of the water or if his candle goes out, he goes back to be recharged and starts again.

Bounce Ball Use five different sizes and types of ball and a large cardboard carton. The players in turn bounce the balls into the carton from a point 3 metres away. Score a point for each ball that goes in the box.

Some ideas for inclusion in outdoor Pack Meetings:

High Jump Two garden canes are stuck into the ground as uprights and the cross-bar is attached by rubber bands which are strong enough to hold it but will snap if any pressure is put on them, i.e. if a boy does not clear the bar.

Long Jump Mark out a length—2 metres, 2.5 metres and 3 metres—and on each one lay a sausage-shaped balloon. Cubs take it in turn to jump, and score 5 points if they reach between 1.75 m and 2.25 m, plus a bonus point if they land on or burst a balloon.

Banana Relay Sixes run a normal relay race but use a banana as a baton. The winning Six receive a box of sweets as a prize or eat all the bananas (if not too squashed!).

Practice tree climbing

Have a cross-country run

Challenge another Pack to a cross-country run

Organise a pram race

Or, if opportunity offers try horse-riding; visit a dry-ski slope; visit an ice-rink, or a roller skating rink; arrange a contest at a bowling alley against a neighbouring Pack.

Encourage Mums with their slimming exercises by suggesting that the Cubs do their own Keep Fit exercises at the same time. Give each boy a chart to mark off each day for a month for himself and Mum!

Codes and Ciphers

Training aids

† *Codes and Ciphers: First Book* by Sam & Beryl Epstein (Franklin Watt Ltd.)

Who might help

Scouters of other Sections of the Group, Venture Scouts, Patrol Leaders or fathers of Cubs

Planning

Older Cub Scouts in particular enjoy activities which include secret codes. Although they do not form part of the Arrow Scheme of training, they can be used to add excitement and intrigue to wide games and Special Pack Meetings.

Right through the ages codes and ciphers have been used to pass information to friends without the contents being understood if the message fell into the wrong hands. Spies and special agents; soldiers, sailors, airmen; Kings and Cub Scouts have all used secret writing.

Most schoolboys will already have tried passing simple messages by substituting one letter of the alphabet for another: A-B, B-C, C-D and so on. Or by writing the alphabet and underneath printing the alphabet backwards, the letters in the bottom line being substituted for those which spell the word in "clear". Each boy can make his own 'key':

A B C D E F G H I J K L M N O P Q R S T U V W X Y Z
Z Y X W V U T S R Q P O N M L K J I H G F E D C B A

Cub Scouts enjoy inventing codes, with a little help from a Scouter. Your Pack might like to have its own code known only to them; if you belong to the 8th Pack, for instance, your code might start with the 8th letter; H would stand for A, I for B, J for C. Or if the boys prefer figures, the key would be: A-8, B-9, C-10, etc.

Not all codes are intended to be kept secret. Some are used to send long messages in such a way that everyone will understand and take action. The best known codes are Morse and Semaphore.

Semaphore, when words are spelt by holding the arms in a certain position to represent the letters, is useful in wide games out of doors, or in camp when one can be seen but cannot be heard. Semaphore is sometimes used by sailors to pass messages from one ship to another.

Morse, a code invented by a man called Samuel F. B. Morse, is even better known and is used internationally. It, too, can be transmitted by flags but more often it is used by telegraph and radio operators, clicking out dots and dashes on a special keyboard.

All Scouts should know S.O.S. (Save our souls) which is sent in Morse by signalling three short dots, followed by three dashes, and three more dots. This is used by mountaineers, yachtsmen, and others, as a sign of distress. The call known as 'May Day' is also a request for help put out by aircraft and ships in need of assistance. This arose from the French 'M'aider' which means 'help me'.

Another way of sending secret messages is by writing the message in invisible ink. This is one of the tests in the Scientist badge, but as it requires very little special knowledge and there are no symbols to remember, it can be enjoyed by younger Cubs as well.

The message is written in one of the invisible inks and when it has dried it will look just like a sheet of ordinary blank paper which no one would suspect contained secret information. The person receiving the paper heats it and the writing will appear. The reason for this (which some of the more scientifically-minded Cub Scouts might like to know!) is that when a sheet of paper containing a message written in invisible ink is heated the compound is broken down by the heat, liberating the element carbon which gives the writing its characteristic brown or blackish colour. Heating requires care. To hold the paper against a lighted 60 watt lamp bulb, or the sole-plate of an electric iron, is preferable to using a naked flame.

Putting it over

Survey Try carrying out your own survey report, to decide which invisible ink the Cubs think is best. They may experiment with milk, lemon, orange or grapefruit juice; vinegar or onion juice; a solution of salt, sugar or washing-soda, or even cola, with which the boys would thoroughly enjoy experimenting.
Simple Picture Code Game Stick on a large sheet of paper a collection of pictures the initial letters of which form the alphabet: (axe, butterfly, chair). Each picture is numbered but not in alphabetical order. Each Six is given a coded message, consisting only of groups of figures. The Cubs decode the message by referring to the Code chart and then carry out the order contained in their message: 'Sit crosslegged', 'Go outside', 'Run into corner'.
Revision An evening of revision of Arrow Skills can be made much more interesting if the instructions are given in code. Send a letter by post to each Sixer during the previous week telling them that on arrival at the Pack Meeting they are to organise the Six to complete a Secret Mission, details of which will be given in code. The Key to the code must be included in the letter. The coded instructions, which they receive on arrival, could concern such activities as: 'Draw the flag of your country', 'Tie the Second to a chair, using a bowline'.
Mystery Outing On an expedition lay out a trail using tracking signs and, at intervals, leave messages of items to collect e.g. an oak leaf, a pebble, a twig—but write these messages in code.

Compass

Training aids

Books

† *Map and Compass Way: Orienteering* by John Disley (Blond Educational)
Out of Doors in Arrow Skills booklet (Gilwell Park)

Compass

The Silva Compass model 7NL is probably the best of the

present 'Silva' range. It has the eight points of the compass clearly marked and so it is useful for Cubs but it can also be used for more advanced work in the Troop. This and other models are available from Scout Shops Ltd.

Who might help

Group Scout Leader and Scout Leader and Assistants
Patrol Leaders
Venture Scouts

Planning

The only real way to learn how to use a compass is to go out of doors and use it, having to rely on it to get back to base. If the Cub Scout has a local knowledge of the area he will obviously not be so reliant on his compass, so it is as well if he can test his skill in unfamiliar country whenever possible, perhaps when on a Pack holiday or expedition.
Activities including the use of a compass represent real adventures to the Cub Scout; for he is beginning to learn how to look after himself when living out of doors and getting about in a strange country, and he will certainly need such skills in the Troop.
Although some compass work can be done indoors in preparation for going out, it is important that the boys should not get the impression that the use of a compass is limited to proving that the piano in headquarters is always in the north, the door is in the east and Red Six corner in the south west.
Show by your own example when using a compass that it is a precision instrument and not a toy, and should be handled with care. At some time in the future the boy's life might depend upon it.

Putting it over

Ideas to use indoors in preparation for going out-of-doors:
Compass directions may be given during the Pack Meeting: 'Stand in Six relay teams at the north end of the hall'.
'Sit on the floor touching the south wall'.
Pictorial compass
On a large sheet of paper draw your headquarters in the centre, then let the Cubs decide which buildings lie along the eight compass directions and draw these on the chart, e.g. school, church, library, Akela's house. Alternatively, mark your

town in the centre and draw a picture to represent countries to the north, south, east and west etc., for example, Eskimos for Iceland, Red Indians for North America, Ski-ing for Norway.

Compass pictures

On squared paper draw an animal or car, or any other simple object with a clear outline. Let the boys try to work out how the picture might be reproduced by using compass directions, e.g. 'Start at the third square from the east on the north edge of the paper, then draw a line south two squares, south-east two squares, west three squares, etc.' The picture resulting

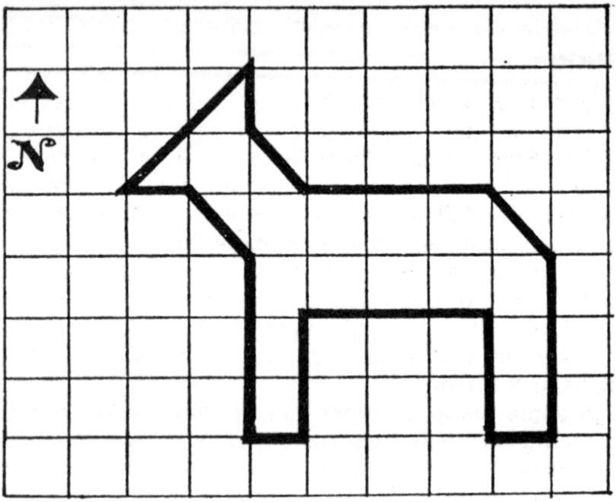

from these directions may bear little resemblance to the original.

Treasure Island

On a large sheet of paper draw a treasure island, mark in north and pin the paper to a polystyrene tile. Cut out several objects to go on the island: a hut, three palm trees, a look-out post, a boat, a chest of treasure.

A story is then read describing the island: The house is built in the north-west point of the island, just to the east of the palm trees, and so on. The Cubs try to place the cut-outs in the appropriate positions on the island. Alternatively, use a camp site with cut-out tents, flagpole, camp fire circle, kitchen, and so on. Or the boys could make their own drawings of the scene, as each object is mentioned in the course of the story.

Draughtboard journey

Again on squared paper, draw a village, positioning each

feature neatly within a square: the village pond, the church, trees, school, shop, post box. The Cub starts at a given point and moves according to directions: 2 squares north, 4—north-east, 3—south, and so on. After a few moves check where the Cub is, having worked it out yourself first. Map symbols might be included in this game.

Activities out-of-doors

On Safari

In an area of woodland lay out a compass trail from your base, round a series of 'posts' and back to base again. Write down the compass directions. At each 'post'—a convenient tree or gate—hide an envelope containing pictures or drawings of wild animals, such as you might see on safari: tigers, elephants, lions, etc. The Sixes are sent off at timed intervals along the trail and as they locate each post they take from the envelope a picture of the animal spotted at that position. The last Six on the trail also removes the envelopes. An adult with each Six is advisable.

Alternatively this could be a 'Mowgli in the Jungle' game and the envelopes would contain pictures of Bagheera, Kaa, Baloo, etc.

Plane crash

The Cubs are led blindfold to a place in the middle of some woodland or scrubland. There each Six is given a card saying 'Your plane has crashed in the middle of the jungle. All around you are swamps, man-eating crocodiles and fierce jungle animals. Before your radio went out of order someone told you that there was only one safe route out of the place and your

navigator wrote this down, e.g. 40 metres north, 10 metres north-west, 3 metres east, etc. Use your compass and follow the "safe route" back to base.
Before playing this game the Cubs must have been given a key for distance: so many paces equal so many metres.

Atomic Power Station

Each Six is part of a team building an atomic power station in a remote part of the country. Each crew must try and get a package of radio-active material to the site within a given time or it becomes unusable. Unfortunately there are no roads in the area and so each crew must follow a simple track to the site, following compass directions. Deduct points for each minute over the time allowance.

Detective

Work out beforehand a compass trail in the immediate surroundings of your headquarters, with each 'leg' of the journey leading to a clue, such as 'Go 25 metres east. Here you will see a strange man in a bowler hat—can you recognise him?' (A figure on an advertisement hoarding). 'Turn to the

south and proceed 50 metres: People have been seen taking secret messages to the building facing you. What is the name of the building?' (The Post Office). '30 metres west is a place often frequented by a wanted man. Write down the name without being seen by the people inside'. (A local cafe, where Akela could have a cup of tea and keep a look out from the window).

Whose home?

Pair off the Sixes (or divide into small groups if you have an odd number). Each Six chooses a member of the other Six and without letting him know, goes and works out the route from headquarters to his home by writing down compass directions. An adult should go with each group. They then return to headquarters and exchange instructions with the other Six, who then follow the directions to find out whose home was chosen.

It might be possible for the adult with the first group to leave a bar of chocolate at the chosen house, which the second group can collect if they follow their instructions properly.

Ways of finding north

Make a wall chart to show all the ways of finding north having set the boys various problems to discuss, such as:

Old churches are usually built on an east to west line with the bell-tower at the west-end. Check on your local church.

The prevailing wind will often shape trees. Look at ones near your headquarters, particularly if you live near the coast, or in an isolated country area. The moss on tree stumps is usually more fertile on the north side since it generally stays damper there; can you find any evidence of this?

Look up at the television aerials. Are they lined up in a particular way? Why is this?

At noon the sun is due south. In what direction would shadows be cast at 6 p.m. (allowing for British Summer time?). Is there a public clock where you could check this?

At night find the Plough and from it find the Pole Star. By drawing an imaginary line from the Pole Star to earth, you can locate north.

The compass should be used to confirm or check all findings.

Cooking

Training aids

Books

Cookery books written for children, or simple recipes from your own books.

Who might help

Ladies of the Group Council
Cubs' Mums

Planning

Just about anything connected with food is guaranteed success with Cub Scouts.

Much will depend on the room in which you meet, but even in a church hall some food can be cooked if adequate preparations are made: newspapers to cover the floor, old shirts with the sleeves cut short to cover the boys, and a fire extinguisher nearby. If there are no cooking facilities in your headquarters it might be possible to borrow the Group's gas stoves, and if that fails there are still some recipes to be tried which need no cooking at all.

Adult supervision will almost certainly be needed, but make sure it is only supervision—don't let them have all the fun while the Cubs are just looking on. This is a good activity for which to ask help from an 'interested' Mum; she will feel she has an important part to play, where it might be more difficult to involve her in knot-tying or flags.

Cooking some special treat for all the Pack to eat at the end of the meeting will keep the interest of the older boys. If they become proficient, they may like to make sweets for sale at the next fund-raising event, or as presents for other people.

Putting it over

Simple recipes:

Tin-top pancakes Celebrate Shrove Tuesday by cooking pancakes on the bottom of a large upturned tin.

Ingredients: $\frac{1}{4}$ lb flour
1 egg
$\frac{1}{2}$ pint milk
a pinch of salt

This should be enough for six small pancakes.
Method: Pierce a series of holes in the sides of the tin about ½ an inch from the open-end, and then stand it over a lighted candle. Grease the base of the tin, which will form your hot-plate, and drop on to it a tablespoonful of pancake mixture, to make a thin pancake. When cooked on one side, carefully turn and cook on the other side.
Spread with jam or syrup before eating.

Chocolate Crispies

Ingredients: A bar of milk chocolate
A packet of breakfast cereal
Paper cake cases

Method: Melt a bar of chocolate in a basin over a pan of hot water. Remove the basin and stir in enough cereal so that they are all covered with chocolate. Put spoonfuls of the mixture into paper cases and leave to set. In about five minutes they will be ready to eat.

Bonfire toffee

Ingredients: ¼ lb demerara sugar
½ oz butter
½ tablespoonful water
½ tablespoonful vinegar
1 tablespoonful treacle

Method: Put all the ingredients into a saucepan. Boil for 15 minutes, or until it hardens when dropped into cold water. Pour into a greased tin and leave to set. (If made at the beginning of the Pack Meeting it should be ready to eat by the end of it. This quantity is more than enough for a Six.)

Coconut ice

Ingredients: ⅓ cup milk and water (you may need less)
½ lb sugar
2 oz desiccated coconut
Pink food colouring

Method: Put milk, water and sugar into a large pan and boil for six minutes. Add the coconut until it thickens. Pour half into a tray lined with aluminium foil. Add a drop of pink food colouring to the remainder and pour on top of the first. Leave to set. (If the mixture is not too wet it should set within the space of a Pack Meeting. This quantity is more than enough for a Six.)

If you have an oven:
Baked cheesy potato Scrub the potatoes well and place in a

medium oven for about half an hour, until soft when touched. In the meantime grate some cheese, add salt and pepper. When the potatoes are cooked, split them open and add some butter and cheese to each one.

Baked apples Wash the apples and carefully remove the cores. Place on a buttered baking tin and fill the holes, left after removal of the core, with a mixture of brown sugar and sultanas or currants. Bake for about 30 minutes at 300° (Reg. 3).

Coconut Pyramids

Ingredients:
- 2 stiffly beaten egg whites
- 6 oz desiccated coconut
- 3 oz caster sugar
- 1 dessertspoonful cornflour
- glacé cherries for decoration

Method: Mix coconut, cornflour and sugar together. Work into egg whites until a firm mixture is obtained. Form into pyramids using a greased egg cup. Bake on a greased baking tin, or rice paper, at 350°C (Reg. 3) until golden brown on top. Handle carefully until cold. Decorate with cherries. (Sufficient for a Six).

Country Code

Training aids

Books

† *Fun with Ecology* by Geoffrey Watson (Kaye and Ward,—help in introducing conservation to children.

Safety in Arrow Skills booklet (Gilwell Park)

Posters and Leaflets

Leaflets, posters and workbooks are available from the Royal Society for the Prevention of Accidents, Safety Education Department, Royal Oak Centre, Brighton Road, Purley, Surrey CR2 2UR and a catalogue and price list is available. Examples are:—

My Country and Seaside Safety Book—Workbook SE30

Walking Safely on Country Roads—Leaflet SE35

These Fruits are Dangerous—Coloured pictorial aid (30in x 20in) HSP87—1

Poisonous Fungi—Coloured pictorial aid (30in x 20in) HSP113—1

Country Code This booklet and various relevant posters are available (some free of charge) from The Countryside Commission, 19-23 Albert Road, Manchester, M19 2EQ

Who might help

Farmers or foresters
Members of Rambler's Clubs
Keep Britain Tidy Group
Leaders from a rural Scout Group

Planning

If we were taking Cub Scouts abroad, we could go to great lengths to explain to them the different customs and ways of life which they would expect to find. Going into the country is, for boys who live in cities, almost like a visit to a strange land. They naturally cannot understand what behaviour is expected of them, without explanation.
Even in the country, where boys may instinctively know and appreciate the need for the Country Code, they tend to take it for granted or to forget it in the excitement of the moment, so an occasional reminder should be included in the programme.

Putting it over

There are so many practical activities, the choice of which must depend partly on the environment and partly on the imagination and enterprise of those who plan:
Clear a ditch—great fun for Cub Scouts in wellington boots.
Plant a tree or some bulbs.
Adopt a stream—keep it flowing throughout the year.
Make a map of local footpaths where it is suitable to take dogs for a walk.

Invite a farmer or a forester to describe how the Country Code helps him in his work.

Tell the story of Johnny Appleseed who spent his life planting apple pips which grew into the vast orchards of Ohio.

Walk part of a National Footpath such as the Pembrokeshire Coast Path. Follow the waymark in the form of an acorn, and report any damage you may find, such as broken fences, stiles or hedges, to the nearest Countryside Commission Information Centre when you return. You could also pick up any litter you find on the way.

Clear a beach of litter particularly the indestructible type—plastic containers, glass bottles, tins.

Have a 'Keep our Beaches Safe' poster competition just before the school holidays.

Make a 'Litter Monster' of litter collected from around your headquarters, and formally bury him in a dustbin.

Discuss the effect of litter on wild-life—a calf or lamb might suffocate, or die through eating a polythene bag. Mice and other small creatures explore the insides of milk bottles thrown into hedges and cannot turn round to get out again, and so perish. Paper can be swept up from street gutters, but it is difficult to pick up from grass or out of hedges.

Compose an anti-litter song dropping off words and substituting actions, to the tune of 'John Brown's Body'.

Keep a chart of birds and flowers seen in your area during the summer. Discuss whether any of them are threatened because of new buildings, motorways or pollution, and, if so, what could be done about this.

If your Pack is a rural one, invite a city Pack to spend a day with you and introduce them to the countryside.

Quick Scavenger Hunt. Find eleven objects whose initial letters spell the words Country Code.

Have a litter-bin competition, decorate large paper sacks, use them on your Pack expeditions to bring your litter home.

Country Code television. Encourage every Cub to illustrate part of the Country Code and then join the pictures together to form a long strip. Fasten this on two pieces of dowelling like a camera film and insert it into a carton with a hole as a television screen. Show your 'film' on a parents' evening and invite them to take part in a competition to write a six-line 'jingle' about the Country Code, to a well-known tune.

Entertaining

Training aids

Books

Miming, Acting, Stage-props, Puppetry and Masks

† *You can Act* by Lewy Olfson (The Oak Tree Press Ltd)
† *Paper Faces* by Michael Grater (Ladybird Books Ltd)
† *Easy to make puppets* by Alan and Brenda Stockwell (Ladybird Books Ltd)
* *A Selection of Sketches and Plays*

Conjuring

† *Magic with Science* by Walter B. Gibson (Wm Collins)
† *My Colour Book of Magic and Simple Tricks* by Clayton James (Schofield and Sims)
Simple Science Experiments by Albert James (Schofield and Sims)
The Puffin Book of Magic by Norman Hunter (Penguin Books)
* *Tricks and Magic* by James Webster (Ladybird Books Ltd)

Singing

* *Cub Scout Songs* by Brian Sims (Brown, Son & Ferguson Ltd)
* *English Folk Songs* (Penguin)
*† *The Scout Fire and Folk Song Book* (The Scout Association)

General

† *Activities for Cub Scouts* (Gilwell Park)

Who might help

The Assistant District Commissioner (Cub Scouts)
Scouters from other Packs
Other Scouters in the Group

Planning

Entertaining in the Pack is more a matter of entertaining ourselves than putting on a polished performance for other people, and, as such, it is another important 'working tool' for Pack Scouters. While enjoying themselves the Cubs will be gaining in self-confidence, and in an appreciation of the talents of others; and often they will be revising some Arrow Badge skills at the same time.

The leader's role is to provide the setting and the stimulus and allow the boys to develop their own creative ideas, without

imposing adult ones. All Cubs should take part, as far as possible. Even the most timid boy can join in by making 'props' or noises off-stage, or may be willing to operate a puppet, where he can hide behind the puppet theatre out of view of the audience.
Simple acting games are a good way to start but should lead on to a variety of activities to discover and encourage the talents of the individuals. You may find in the end that you have a 'mini-show' which would delight parents and friends, as boys of Cub Scout age have a natural charm and appeal on-stage. But it will involve much hard work and rehearsal if it is decided to put on a public performance, as the standard on such occasions must be the very best that can be produced. Always insist on courteous attention to whoever is performing, as that is also an important part of the training.

Putting it over

Acting Games In turn, the Sixes act a song title or a book title, or an Arrow activity, while the others guess what it is.
Play charades Work out a few suitable words in readiness.
Act situations Give a group or an individual secret orders for them to act: 'You have spilt a jar of jam on the carpet and are trying to clean up the mess before your Mother, who is already coming down the road, reaches home.'
'The chain has come off the bicycle of your Brownie friend and you gallantly offer to help, but it proves a more difficult job than you had imagined.'
'Three of you are putting up a large tent on a very windy day.'
Arrow work involving acting:
Act the stories of the saints, or an incident involving home safety, road safety, water safety, Country Code, or first aid.

Act an incident from 'The Story of Baden-Powell', using the tape recording of this name to give background effects.

Act an incident involving the Promise and Law.

Tell a yarn, but stop before the conclusion and ask the Cubs to act out how they think the story ended.

Depict, as a series of tableaux, some events from local history.

Role-play a real life situation which Cub Scouts might face, in order to help them make decisions and establish their own values and standards: 'Your friends who are not Cub Scouts ask you to go on a shop-lifting spree, and call you a "sissy" if you won't join in. What would you do?'

Act a Bible story or tale of heroism, suitable for use at the end of the evening before prayers, or at an Act of Worship.

Give each Six a title 'What happened at Cooper's Creek', or 'Cub Scout Peter's lucky escape', and ask them to make up a 5 minute play based on this title. Each Six then performs their play to the rest of the Pack.

Hold a Fun month Each week the members of one Six are each asked to tell a joke. This could be good training in speaking, in self-confidence—or maybe in self-control!

Story-telling Provide opportunities for boys who have visited any unusual place or event to tell the Pack about it, or for a boy working for the Book Reader badge to give a shortened version of one of the books he has read.

Poetry may not play a very large part in Pack Meetings but a few simple lines may be used with telling effect during an Act of Worship. On other occasions the more humourous type of verse or limericks are enjoyed by boys.

The Camp Fire Sketches which make us groan as we see them for the umpteenth time, still provide great amusement for Cub Scouts.

Back-room boys Behind every star performer there are a number of back-room boys to build scenery, make 'props', provide realistic noises off-stage, design advertising posters, and many other important jobs. Cubs of the less extrovert type may show a real flair in one of these jobs.

Puppetry Children never seem to tire of puppets, and they can vary from the simplest paper-bag puppet to the very elaborate stringed variety. Apart from their entertainment value, they help build up a boy's confidence in speaking, and can be used to reinforce much of our Arrow Training—by making puppets and putting on a play about Water Safety, or Scouting history, or St. George rescuing the maiden from the dragon. There are many different types of puppets with which to experiment:

Paper bag or box puppets

Puppets made from an old rolled-up sock
Dish-mop puppets
Ping pong ball puppets
Finger puppets
Puppets made from balsa-wood, or paper mâché—these are usually more carefully made, fashioned to portray a character, and dressed accordingly.

These are all hand or glove puppets and are fairly easy to manipulate. Except for the first three, they are manipulated by one finger guiding the head and two other fingers guiding the puppet's arms. There are no feet as the costume is made long enough to cover the arm down to the elbow. A baby's cast-off tee-shirt is often a useful size for a puppet's cloak.

A more advanced type of puppet is known as a marionette. It is jointed and worked by string from its head, arms and legs. They can often be seen on television programmes and, although within the capabilities of boys, require much more patience and expertise to make and use effectively, and so are best suggested as an individual project to a boy who is particularly keen on puppetry.

A folding puppet theatre, or a very large cardboard packing case with a hole cut in one side, will be needed. Some boys will enjoy painting suitable backcloths or making scenery.

Shadow puppets provide a rather different type of approach. The silhouettes of the various characters are cut out of stiff black paper, which is slotted into the ends of thin canes in order that they may be held up against a screen. A bright light behind the screen projects the shadows. It is possible to make some movable parts, or, to give added impact to the main characters, parts of the black paper may be cut out and the holes covered with coloured cellophane which will appear as bright spots of colour on the screen. This technique can also be used to represent lighted windows in buildings.

Shadow puppets often have a whimsical air about them, and can be used effectively to tell folk-stories or legends, or even, with a little practice, to illustrate Bible stories as part of an Act of Worship.

People Puppets This is an art of the mummers of old and can give a lot of fun to the young. Paper sacks, thoroughly cleaned, must be large enough to cover the upper half of the boy, with holes cut for his eyes. The various 'characters' in the play may be portrayed by decorating the sacks with felt-tipped pens or pieces of paper stuck on to give a 3-D effect.

Masks Though not really puppets in the proper sense of the word, the idea of making face masks and acting a play follows on from the idea of people puppets. These also encourage a shy boy as he feels he cannot be recognised when hiding behind his mask. Perhaps Hallowe'en is a good time to try out mask-making.

Tumbling tricks if carried out with precision, can be good entertainment and will appeal to the more agile members of the Pack.

Dancing Sword or Maori stick dances are popular with boys, as they imagine themselves as young warriors. They require performers with a good sense of rhythm.

Conjuring tricks are beloved of small boys and there are plenty of books giving ideas which do not require special equipment, except perhaps the inevitable magic wand. It is a good plan for one leader to work 'in secret' with just two or three boys to develop a series of tricks with which to intrigue the Pack, as it is this intrigue and mystery which adds greatly to the conjurer's art, together with his particular form of patter.

Musical instruments Encourage any young musicians in the Pack to bring their instruments along occasionally and play

for the other Cubs. A Pack may take pride in its own band with home-made instruments: 'bongo' drums, 'pop' bottle top rattles, shakers, milk bottle xylophones, 'tubular' bells using different sized nails, whistles, cigar box guitars, bull roarers, cymbals. Attempts to play these simple instruments will help the Cub Scouts to appreciate the real musical talents of others.

Take just a few boys who are really interested, to an orchestral concert. Sit where they can get a good view of the instrumentalists and choose a programme which is likely to appeal to them.

Singing There is a saying that a 'singing Pack is a happy Pack' and it does seem to work out that way. Build up the Pack's repertoire of songs by singing just a couple of songs at the close of each Pack Meeting; it is not necessary always to have a full scale sing-song.

If the Pack is not in the habit of singing, a good beginning would be to ask the Sixers' Council to introduce some of the 'pop' songs which they know: 'Happy Wanderer', 'Yellow Submarine', or whatever may be popular at the moment.

Ask the Scout Leader or Group Scout Leader to teach the Pack some Scouting songs known by the rest of the Group: 'I've got that B.-P. spirit,' 'We're on the Scouting trail' and some popular Yells.

Ask a Scouter from another Pack, or the Assistant District Commissioner (Cub Scouts), to introduce some songs enjoyed by other Cub Scouts. Have a joint sing-song with a neighbouring Pack and exchange songs.

Learn a song in a foreign language to welcome a guest from overseas, or sing on an international evening.

Encourage any soloists in the Pack to sing occasionally. Those who are choir boys may not be as nervous as you imagine, as they will have had practice of singing before a crowd. Boys of Cub age often have lovely singing voices so don't let all your songs be rowdy ones—include a few which are suitable for Acts of Worship. Some of the modern religious music and hymn tunes may be better known by Cub Scouts than the more traditional music and you should bear this in mind when making your choice.

Develop a Pack song book in which favourite rounds, action songs and yells, are written down, as it is sc easy to forget the words just when you need them. Take your song book with you on Pack expeditions and holidays, and lead a few songs whilst sitting down after a picnic lunch, or waiting for a bus; or on a wet day in camp, or to quieten the Cubs down before bed-time.

Exploring

Training aids

Books

† *Townlook 1* by Gordon S. Boon

† *Townlook 2* by Kenneth Lindley (Pergammon Press)

Let's Explore books about individual buildings, often available in cathedrals, contain puzzles and pictures to colour.

I-Spy series (Model and Allied Publications Ltd)

In the Street	*Signs and Symbols*
On the Road	*Buses and Coaches*
Sights of London	*History*
Churches	*On a car journey*
	On a train journey

Ladybird Series (Ladybird Books Ltd)

The Story of our Churches and Cathedrals

The Story of Houses and Homes

The Story of Lighthouses, Lightships and Lifeboats

* *London*

* *Understanding Maps*

What to look for inside a church

What to look for outside a church

Special Days and Customs

The Shire Series (Shire Publications)

Discovering English Customs and Traditions

Discovering England's Trees

Discovering Windmills

Exploring in Arrow Skills booklet (Gilwell Park)

Teacher's Guide

† *Out and About*—a teacher's guide to safety on educational visits. Published for the Schools Council by Evans/ Methuen Educational Press

Cards

* Scoutaids Series CBC 3 *24-hour Clock*

Who might help

Museum curator
History teacher
Verger of local church
Warden of any local ancient buildings
Group Scout Leader—help with small group of boys
Assistant District Commissioner (Cub Scouts)

Planning

This is not an indoor activity, it is essentially something to be done out of doors, though obviously there is some preparatory work that can be done inside your headquarters.

It is mainly an activity to be carried out in small groups, for a Pack of thirty Cub Scouts 'exploring' a Nature Reserve, a cathedral or a museum, can easily spoil the pleasure of any other members of the public who happen to be there on the same day. It is also easier to keep an eye on a small group of younger Cub Scouts when they are finding out the whereabouts of the essential services in the locality.

The more involved a boy becomes in finding his own way about, the more confident he will grow. This activity is good preparation for Scouting and Venture Scouting, as it gives a boy the idea of exploring his own locality which can later be extended further afield in other parts of the country, and eventually abroad.

Such activities should, however, be carefully supervised even though the boys may not be aware of the supervision.

Putting it over

A large model of your area including the most important buildings might be made in polystyrene and then painted.

On a large scale street map (often available from estate agents) mark the essential services, local schools, churches, your headquarters, any ancient buildings or other places of interest; also the main bus routes, or railway lines.

'Who's Who' To compile a useful reference book of your own locality, calls for a different type of exploring, providing such information as the name and number of the policeman on whose beat your headquarters is; the name of the nearest doctor, and what the letters after his name mean. Who is the Chief Fire Officer? What can you find out about the fire engines he controls: makes of engine, power, capacity of pumps? What are the names of the clergymen in your area? Were any of them Scouts? Find out the name of your local librarian. What kind of training was required for that job?

Make a scrapbook to include any special features of your locality, such as a rubbing of a car number plate which has the local registration letters; a drawing of a shirt, shorts and socks, painted in the colours of the nearest large football club; any bill-heads, wrapping paper or paper bags from the nearest row of shops, together with a note of the commodities each shop sells.

To these might be added a postcard of any features which are of particular interest to visitors, and drawings of any local monuments or memorials, Inn signs, or coat of arms.

Finally a picture of a Cub Scout wearing the Group Scarf, a

Group name-tape and a District badge with the signature of the Group Scout Leader and District Commissioner would complete the collection.

Puzzle Pictures Photographs or slides of well-known features in the district but taken from unusual angles, can provide an interesting competition, perhaps for a Parents' Evening.

Describe some well-known local features on tape such as: 'A building dating from 1930, mostly of brick, used largely by children', might be the local school. 'A stone building, the only one of this design in the district, with a coat-of-arms carved above the doorway', might be the Church.

The Cubs can play the cassette on a portable tape recorder and try to solve the clues.

Directing a stranger Each Cub in a small group is given a card bearing the name of a place in the district, and each in turn must direct a foreigner from headquarters to the place on the card without speaking, but by miming, or drawing directions; the other boys try to work out the destination.

Mathematical Quiz Each Six is given instructions and is provided with a paper and pencil, a note of the time limits, and if possible a Scouter to each Six. They should know where to find a telephone directory.

The instructions might include problems such as the following:

1. On the monument in the Market Square, you will find carved the date when it was erected. Add the separate numbers of this date together.

2. Add to this the number of collections from the Post Office on Saturday.

3. Add to this the number of the house on High Street where Mr. Smith, the taxi proprietor, lives.

4. Take away from the total so far the number of the bus which runs along this route.

5. Add together the separate numbers in Dr. Black's telephone number, and add this to your total.

6. Find out the shop number of the chemist who opens late on Fridays, and multiply your total by this number.

7. Subtract from the total so far the number of new pence in a £, and then add on the number of new pence required to make an emergency phone call.

8. Add together the number of holes in a telephone dial, the number of figures in a local telephone number and take it away from the total so far.

9. Add together the digits of the number to be dialled in an emergency, when telephoning to call the police, ambulance or fire brigade, and add it to your total.

10. Divide by 20, and the number remaining is the number of a house in Church Street, which has a letter for you pinned behind its front gate.
The letter should direct the group back to the headquarters adding:
'To know your district was your quest
Now ask Akela for the Treasure Chest.'
Visit the nearest railway station, coach station, airport or harbour. Arrange for someone who works there to explain their job, and the work of the place. Make a model of it afterwards.
Beat the Parish Bounds It might be an interesting activity for youngsters to carry out this ancient custom of walking round the boundaries of a parish, which was done in order to confirm the exact extent of the land owned.

Fire Lighting

Training aids

Books

† *Activities for Cub Scouts* (Gilwell Park)

Who might help

Patrol Leaders
Scout Leaders and the Group Scout Leader
Camp site Warden
Members of the local Service Team

Planning

Perhaps of all the activities the boys enjoy during their time with the Pack, the most popular one is lighting a fire and cooking a sausage on it. These are the Scouting activities which appeal so much to small boys, and cannot be matched even by the most exciting programmes indoors. Also he is unlikely to do such things at school, which adds to their attraction.

But firelighting is not as easy as it looks, and so preparations must be made so that each boy does get a fire going and is able to keep it alight, or disappointment will cloud the day.
Safety precautions must obviously be observed and care taken to extinguish all fires properly afterwards.

Putting it over

In these days of central heating, electric fires and cookers, many children will never have handled matches.
Demonstrate how to strike a match Most grown-ups strike matches towards themselves, but we train children to strike matches away from themselves as there is less danger of them setting fire to their own clothing that way. *Always use safety matches.*
Candle lighting relay (To give practice in handling matches) Each Six has a candle in a candlestick and a box of safety matches. The Sixes line up in relay formation with an adult to supervise each Six. The Sixer begins by striking a match and lighting the candle. He then carries it to the other end of the room, blows out the candle and returns to his Six taking 'pins-and-needles' steps, i.e. putting one foot in front of the other, the back of one heel touching the toe of the other foot. Penalty points against the Six are incurred if a boy has to use more than one match, if the candle goes out whilst he is carrying it, or if he does not return in the prescribed manner. The winners are the ones with the least number of penalty points. Emphasis should be on careful handling of the matches and lighted candles. The evening might end by lighting all the candles and using them as an indoor 'camp fire' for a brief sing-song.
Make posters to show safety rules when firelighting. Use such items as an empty match box cover, twigs, red crêpe paper or red foil for flames, and a small amount of water in a polythene bag.
Make a training aid to show details of the trees which supply the best wood for firelighting, choosing those which can be found near the place where fires are to be lit, so that they are easily recognised. Show the shape of the tree in summer and winter, its leaves and fruit, its twigs and bark. This can also be linked with a Bronze Arrow Nature activity, although for fire-lighting, boys must be taught to use only dead wood.
Model fires Take some twigs of different thicknesses to the Pack Meeting before an expedition and let the Cubs build model fires on a plasticine base with twigs about as thin as a match.

Most boys tend to make the error of using twigs which are too thick and have difficulty getting them to light so this early introduction will save time on the expedition itself.
Cooking Sausages It does not matter which method of cooking sausages the Cubs use, so long as they can eat them afterwards!

Survey After experimenting with various methods produce a Survey report: those cooked in a frying pan may be more edible, but those cooked on a stick over the embers are more fun to do. If the sausages are wrapped in aluminium foil before they are put on the stick, it should prevent them becoming too smoked or blackened. Hot embers are essential for successful cooking so allow enough time for wood to reach this stage before beginning to cook.
Extinguishing fires Ask a fireman to talk to the Pack about forest fires and show a few pictures if possible. Make a collage to urge people to be sure to put out fires properly, and not to throw cigarette ends away carelessly. Ask an outsider to visit the site as you are clearing up to try and detect where the Cubs have had fires. Perhaps a small prize can be given to any boys whose fireplace cannot be found.

Fishing

Training aids

Books

Coarse Fishing by N. Scott (Ladybird Books Ltd)

Who might help

Other leaders in the Group
Lay helpers
Parents who enjoy fishing as a pastime

Planning

Some of your Cubs may already be keen fishermen. Certainly if there is a suitable river, pond, lake or stretch of coast nearby, most boys in the Pack will try fishing at some time or another. You can share their interest, even if you have no desire to take them fishing, by helping them to make floats, or to recognise different species of fish or find out about the 'closed' season or times of tides. You can certainly help them to carry out their fishing adventures safely by ensuring that they know the water safety rules and understand the reasons behind them.

Putting it over

Have a fisherman's evening making floats from cocktail sticks and corks (see Ladybird book for details). Paint them in bright colours on top so that they can be seen when bobbing about on top of the water, and dark green or black underneath so that they merge with the water.

Have a casting competition (obviously without hooks on the lines). Each boy might have three casts, which must be marked, the best distance scoring, or the one that gets nearest to a marker. A sugar fish might be awarded to the one who gets closest to the target.

Show the Cubs how to do whipping so that they can carry out professional-looking repairs to their rods. Try making rods from garden canes, for boys who do not have a proper rod but would like to try fishing.

Pin up pictures of fish which can be caught in your locality and have a competition to find out who can name the most. The winner explains the special features of each fish which aid recognition.

Teach the Cubs the special knots which are required to hold nylon lines securely—the double blood knot, the half blood knot, the whipping bend, the double overhand loop knot and the two loop knot. (All these are illustrated clearly in the Ladybird book *Coarse Fishing.)*

Discuss the merits of places to fish locally then discuss any special hazards to fishermen at those places—slippery river banks, line easily gets caught up in low overhanging branches, the tide comes in quickly and cuts off the route back to the cliff top, the hook can get caught up in seaweed. Talk over what one should do in such circumstances, and how to help others who have got into difficulties.

Have an early morning fishing expedition ending with a breakfast of bacon and eggs cooked out of doors.
Have a pond-dipping expedition Chart your pond and show the depth of the water, the insects, fish and other wild life that live in or on the pond, the plants which grow in it, the trees which grow round it. Take some spare clothing, just in case someone becomes too enthusiastic!

Flags and Saints

Training aids

Books

Ladybird Series (Ladybird Books Ltd)
* *Flags*
* *A First Book of Saints*
The Story of Captain Cook
* *Penguin Dictionary of Saints* by Donald Attwater (Penguin Books Ltd)
*† *Observer's Book of Flags* (Frederick Warne & Co. Ltd)
Flags & Countries in Arrow Skills booklet (Gilwell Park)

Cards

* *Flag and Emblem Cards* Set of 16 cards illustrating the national flags and emblems of Great Britain
Composition of the Union Flag card (The Girl Guides Association)

Who might help

Group Scout Leader
Assistant District Commissioner (Cub Scouts)
District Commissioner
Venture Scouts

Planning

This Arrow activity area is a vast one, providing a wealth of opportunities to make history 'come alive'. It should never degenerate into a parrot-fashion repetition of dates and names in order to pass a test.

Putting it over

The Royal Family
Each Six is asked to bring to the next meeting two or three questions about the Royal Family. These are handed in at the start of the meeting to a leader, who checks that the facts are correct and that none of the questions have been duplicated. The Sixes in turn ask their questions of the other Sixes, who write down the answers. The Sixer of the Six with most correct answers has the honour of lowering the flag at the end of the meeting and breaking it the next week.

Likes and Dislikes Each Six imagines what it must be like to be a member of the Royal Family, and writes a list of all the things they would enjoy about the position; visits abroad, launching a ship, sitting in the Royal Box at the Cup Final.

The things they would not like so much, such as: having to look cheerful even if they might not feel like it, not being able to go anywhere without being photographed, having to be on their best behaviour all the time.

Royal transport poster Build up a poster over a month of all the various forms of transport used by members of the Royal Family: the Royal Yacht 'Britannia', aeroplane of the Queen's Flight, a horse, a helicopter, the State Coach, the Royal Landaus, etc.

The National Anthem might be sung—or, for a change, said—at the end of the Pack Meeting nearest to the Queen's Birthday, explaining that it is really a prayer for Her Majesty.

National Anthem Jigsaw Write the first verse of the National Anthem on a piece of thick white card, leaving plenty of space between each line. On the reverse side draw, in correct detail, the Union Flag. Cut up the card so that there is one line of the National Anthem on each piece. The Cub puts the pieces together, and when he thinks they are in the right order he can turn the whole thing over, and it will be obvious if any line is wrongly placed as the lines of the flag will not meet correctly.

The Union Flag The composition calls for plenty of drawing games, or making folding models, which need considerable ingenuity.

Draw a picture or make a model of any buildings on which the Cub Scouts have ever seen the Union Flag flying.

Make a miniature flagpole complete with halyards, capable of taking a small Union Flag, often sold as a cycle pennant. Practise hoisting, breaking and lowering the flag with it.

Explain that the Union Flag flown upside down is a sign of distress.

Tell the story of Jack Jones and then let some of the Cubs act it:

'Jack Jones was a ship's boy, and on one voyage his ship was boarded by pirates. They bound up the crew and hid them below decks. The pirates didn't want anyone to get suspicious, and so they ordered Jack to hoist the Union Flag at the masthead. Jack did not dare disobey but he decided to fly the flag upside down as a sign of distress. He knew that the pirates were hardly likely to notice, but that the Navy would spot the mistake and realise something was wrong and come to their aid, which they did. So Jack Jones saved the crew and the ship, and some say that the Union Flag is often referred to as the Union "Jack" to commemorate his brave act.'

Flags on Stamps Encourage keen stamp collectors to bring any stamps with flags on them to show to the Pack. Pinpoint their country on a map of the world. Find out if there are Cub Scouts in those countries.

Flag Quiz (Supply a copy of the *Observer's Book of Flags,* to help the Cub Scouts discover details of flags they do not know).

1. We call it the Flag but Cubs in other countries use different names: De Vlag, Le Drapeau, Die Fahne. What languages would they be speaking?
2. Which country has a large red maple leaf on its flag?
3. The Jamboree in 1971 was held in a country called 'The Land of the Rising Sun' and its flag represents a red sun on a white field. Which country is this?
4. The 'Star of David' has been associated with the Jews since the Middle Ages. Which country uses this symbol in blue on its flag? Have you even seen this symbol on a building?
5. Only one country has a square flag—which is this?
6. The cedar tree mentioned in the Bible is depicted on one country's flag. Name the country. One particular variety of the tree is also known by this name. Can you find out the names of the other varieties of cedar? Do any of them grow in your area?
7. One flag is known as 'the Stars and Stripes'. The thirteen stripes represent the thirteen original states which formed the 'Union', and the stars represent the number of states at present in the 'Union'. Which country is this?
8. Cub Scouts who live in the Southern Hemisphere can see four stars in the sky called the Southern Cross, which cannot be seen by people living in the Northern Hemisphere. One country depicts these four stars in red on their flag—which country is this?

9. On another flag you will find a laurel wreath surrounding a map of the world—to whom does this flag belong? Why did they include a laurel wreath?
10. Which flag has five inter-linked circles on it? What do these represent?

Answers
1. Dutch, French, German.
2. Canada.
3. Japan.
4. The Republic of Israel.
5. Switzerland.
6. Lebanon.
7. United States of America.
8. New Zealand.
9. United Nations—as a symbol of peace.
10. The Olympic Games Flag—the five continents.

Towns of the British Isles
Ask each Cub to spot 5 different car numbers and bring them to the next meeting. Using a plastic map stencil (sold in stationers or toy shops), draw the British Isles, one copy for each Six. Cut them up into about twelve jigsaw pieces. At the next meeting give each Six a 'jigsaw map', polystyrene tile, some ordinary straight pins and some pins with coloured heads, and an Automobile Association handbook.
Each Six makes its jigsaw, pinning the pieces in place with straight pins. They then check in the A.A. Book the car registration numbers they spotted, and decide from which towns the vehicles come. A check on the maps in the book will help them to locate those towns and insert a pin with a coloured head in those places on their jigsaw. They should then be able to answer such questions as: Who spotted the car from farthest away? What was the town from which most cars came? Has anyone in the Pack visited any of these towns?

Expeditions to places connected with the Saints
St. George—St. George's Chapel, Windsor Castle, Berks. The National Queen's Scout Parade takes place there each year. The choir contains the stalls and brasses of the Garter Knights. There are tombs of many Kings, including those of Henry VIII, Charles I and Edward VII.
St. Patrick—is believed to be buried near Downpatrick, and the Pack could visit the church there and the river up which St. Patrick is said to have sailed; or Slemish mountain, in Co. Antrim, where it is said he tended his sheep.
St. Andrew—Athelstaneford. There is a memorial in the

churchyard at Athelstaneford in East Lothian, above which is always flown the national flag of Scotland, the write saltire on a blue background. The inscription on the plaque reads:

'Tradition says that near this place in times remote Pictish and Scottish warriors about to defeat an army of Northumbrians, saw against a blue sky a great white cross like Saint Andrew's, and in its image made a banner which became the flag of Scotland'.

It would be courteous to write to The Manse of Athelstaneford, North Berwick, East Lothian, for permission to visit, and from whom a descriptive leaflet can be obtained.

St. David—St. David's, Pembrokeshire. A beautiful cathedral which contains the 13th century shrine of St. David. Nearby are the remains of the Bishop's Palace. To the west lies the picturesque Whitesand Bay sheltered by St. David's Head, and about two miles away overlooking Ramsey Round is the lifeboat station, which houses 'Joseph Soar'—the lifeboat which protects the highly dangerous and difficult coast around St. David's Head.

The Stories of the Saints provide endless material for yarns, play-acting, puppet plays and shadowgraph plays. Try not to give the Cub Scouts an impression of the Saints as old men flapping about in white nighties, for they were really very manly characters. Yarns should show how skilled they were in many Scouting techniques: camping, cooking, finding their way over unknown territory, swimming, first aid, knotting, firelighting, etc.

Special Pack Meetings can be planned based on the stories of the Saints, and held on their special days. It might be possible to prepare for these by making:

a collage of the stories of legends of the Saints
a dramatic tape recording of the stories
a shadowgraph of the stories.

St. George

—a Roman Chariot Relay Race

—dress a member of each Six as a Roman Soldier, using crêpe paper, cardboard for shields,

—display a brass rubbing of a knight in armour, take a rubbing of coins, particularly those with heraldic devices on them.

St. Patrick

—Play an adaptation of sheep dog trials (see *Cub Scout Games)*

—Cut out paper shamrocks, number each one of its three leaves, then divide into the three separate pieces. These are

scattered all over the room and each Six tries to collect as many complete shamrocks as possible.
Use the prayer known as 'St. Patrick's Breastplate' to close the meeting.
St. David
—Building a Cathedral relay race using spills to be carried one at a time and laid out in a pre-arranged order. Points for speed and accuracy.
—Play a game on the lines of 'Rock Hurling' (see *Cub Scout Games)*, one side being Welsh soldiers, and making leeks from rolled newspaper to wear as their badge.
St. Andrew
—Magnetic fishing
—Potted Highland Games, throwing the discus (a paper plate), tossing the caber (drinking straw), throwing the hammer (balloon on a string). Each Six to represent a different clan.
—Saved by the Thistles, paper thistles are scattered on the floor in front of teams. Sixers call out compass directions in turn to each blindfold Cub who tries to reach the other end of the room. Any who tread on a thistle are 'captured'.

Handcrafts

Training aids

There are a great many books on handcrafts available today, and the following list covers only a few which leaders might find useful. Some of the books are expensive but may be obtained from Public Libraries which usually have a good selection.

Books

* *Things to Make* (Ladybird Books Ltd)
Something to Do by Septima (Penguin Books)—ideas for each month of the year
* *Origami* by Robert Harbin (Hodder and Stoughton)
* *Mobiles* by Peter Mytton-Davies (Ward Lock)
80 Things to make in cardboard by Janet and Alex D'Amato (Odhams)
† *Everyday Treasures* (Mills and Boon)
† *Holiday Treasures* (Mills and Boon)
† *Make Pop-up Greetings Cards* by Eric Kenneway (Mills and Boon)

Take an Egg Box by R. Slade (Faber and Faber)
† *Introducing Fabric Collage* by Margaret Connor (Batsford)
† *Net Making For All* by Charles Holdgate (Mills and Boon)
† *Paper Faces* by Michael Grater (Mills and Boon)
† *Paper People* by Michael Grater (Mills and Boon)
† *Make it in Paper* by Michael Grater (Mills and Boon)
† *One Piece of Paper* by Michael Grater (Mills and Boon)
† *Paper Play* by Michael Grater (Mills and Boon)
† *You Can Draw Too* by Erich Holle (Blackie)
† *You Can Draw People* by Erich Holle (Blackie)

Cards

† *Lively Craft Cards* by Peter Williams (Mills and Boon)
Set 1 *Using Waste Materials*
Set 2 *Making Musical Instruments*
Set 3 *Models from Cardboard Tubes*
Set 4 *Seasonal Activities*
Set 5 *Look, it works*
Spears Project Cards (Key Facts (U.K.) Ltd)
Outdoor Toys
Toys for Boys
Toys that Work
Space Station
Fun with Arts and Crafts
Puppets

Handcraft Materials

The following supply, by post, a variety of materials, please write for details.
Fred Aldous Ltd., P.O. Box 135, 37 Lever Street, Manchester M60 14X.
Allcraft, 11 Market Street, Watford, Herts.
Arnold & Co., Butterley Street, Leeds, West Yorks.
Dryad Ltd., Northgates, Leicester.

Suppliers of:

Balsa Wood— Solarbo Ltd., Commerce Way, Lancing, Sussex. (Also has some leaflets showing how to construct various items from Balsa wood.)
Matchsticks and Matchboxes— Bryant & May Ltd., Fairfield Road, Bow, London. For matchsticks (without heads) and new empty boxes.

Information on Adhesives— Copydex Ltd., 1 Torquay Street, Harrow Road, London, W2 5BR. Teachers' leaflets.
— Gloy Schools Service, Associated Adhesive Ltd. Eighth Avenue Works, Manor Park, London E.12.

Who might help

Local teachers
Parents and friends with an interest in a particular form of handcrafts
Other Pack Scouters—for exchange of ideas
Assistant District Commissioner (Cub Scouts)—for information on local resources and ideas

Planning

So much has been written about handcrafts for children that you may be bewildered and wonder how to begin to introduce it into your Pack; or you may do lots of handcrafts with your Cubs and just be looking for new ideas. Neither situation will be helped by an attempt in this book to produce a 'blueprint': only you can decide what is right for your Pack. But we can pose a few questions which might help you to make a decision, and add some ideas which may be new to you.

Is it to be a handcraft evening for all the boys in the Pack? Then it must be something reasonably simple and easy to supervise.

Are you allowed 'to make a mess'? If not, then go for something that doesn't need glue or paint.

Who can put over the idea: any of the Pack Scouters, or must someone else be brought in?

Does it work? To be sure, try it yourself at home first, checking the time taken to complete it—don't forget to add on a safety margin as the boys will probably work much slower than you.

Is it something the Cub Scouts will enjoy making, or are you imposing on them your own favourite craft? Ask the Sixers' Council.

Has it been tried at school recently? Ask the local teacher for advice on this.

Are articles being made for sale? If so, are they really worth the money you will be asking for them, and not likely to fall to pieces? Ask a more cynical friend for an opinion, a Cub's Mum often has a biased view. If not for sale, what will the boys do with the result? It will bring more pleasure if it can be used for some practical purpose, or even as a toy or decoration.

Are you making the best use of modern materials? Take a walk round a large do-it-yourself store.

Is the particular handcraft you propose to introduce challenging enough? Are ten-year olds still sticking egg boxes together? Remember they probably went through that stage at play-school!

What about the development of the individual boy? Must every-one do the same thing, or is there opportunity for each boy to explore various ideas, using his own creative instincts and imagination? Are the boys aiming at high standards, finding real pleasure in achievement and in pleasing other people?

Putting it over

Simple handcrafts for younger Cub Scouts:

Make a mobile of jungle animals, cut out of thin card or a polystyrene tile. Akela provides templates, the cut-out animals are coloured and hung, using string and wire coat-hangers.

Make 'pop-up' greetings cards

Things to make and play with:

Robots Working in pairs, the boys try to construct a robot, using large cardboard cartons, or packaging material. Successful models may be equipped with batteries and bulbs to make his eyes light up.

Hexaflexagons and magic-boxes A follow-up from Origami. After the paper has been folded to make a hexaflexagon or 'magic boxes', the various faces are decorated with flags or the water safety rules, to make them into training aids. *See opposite and on next page.*

Pack Band Make musical instruments, and play tunes in which all can take part.

Dioramas Many boys possess an action toy for which a variety of equipment can be obtained. A group of boys could be involved in making a variety of settings: a mountain with a ski-slope made from crumpled chicken wire covered with papier mâché; or a camp site complete with tents fixed to a poly-styrene base: or an imaginative underwater sea-scape complete with buried treasure, for him to explore.

Crazy golf Using large cardboard cartons, plastic bottles and tins, construct a 'crazy golf' course (as often seen at the seaside or in parks). Each Six can make two pieces and then they are all laid out to form a course, and the Open Golf

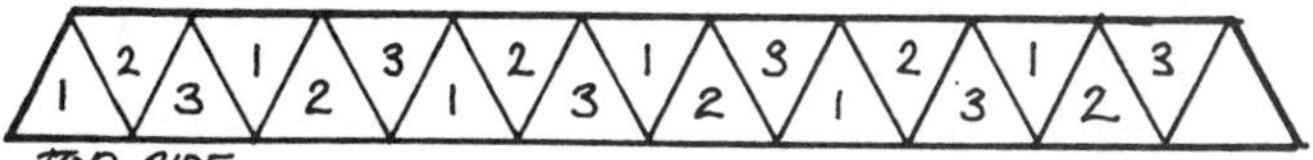

TOP SIDE

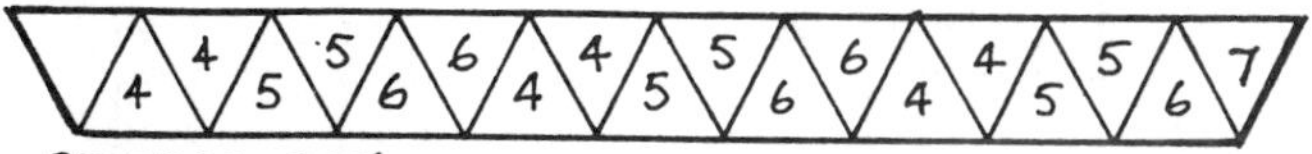

REVERSE SIDE

FOLD 4 ON TO 4, 5 ON TO 5 AND SO ON ALONG THE LENGTH OF STRIP:—

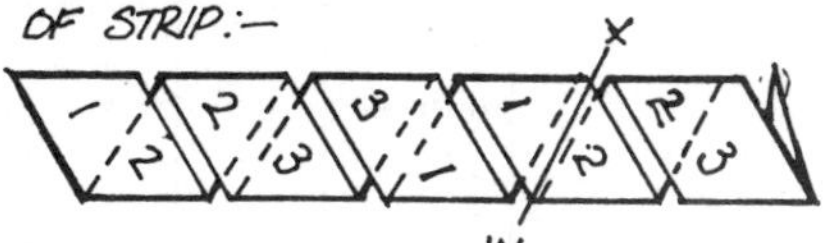

FOLD BACK ALONG LINE WX

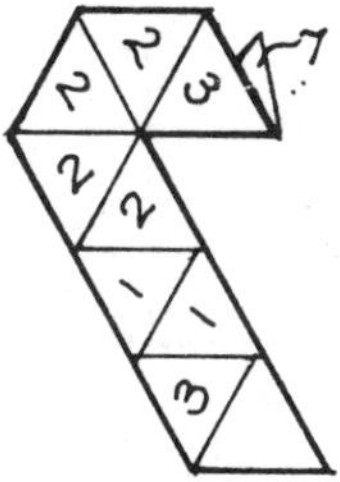

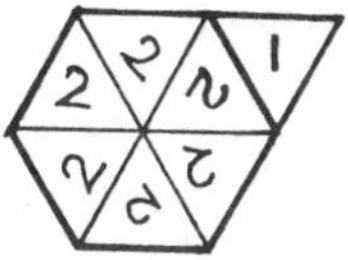

GLUE FACES 1 and 7 TOGETHER.

1 PINCH TWO ADJACENT TRIANGLES TOGETHER
2 PUSH OPPOSITE POINT DOWNWARDS
3 PULL DOWN FROM CENTRE RELEASING INITIAL GRIP

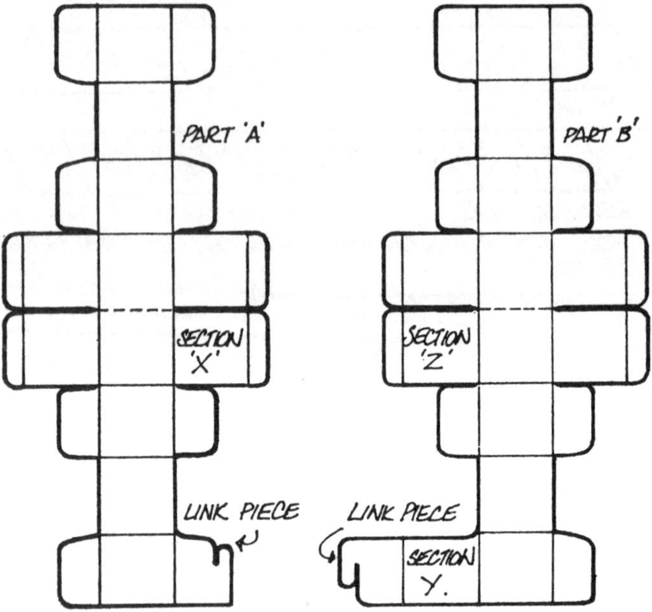

PART 'A' AND PART 'B' EACH MAKE TWO BOXES, THE AREAS EITHER SIDE OF THE DOTTED LINE EACH MAKING ONE BOX. THE CARDS SHOULD BE FOLDED IN THE SAME DIRECTION ON EACH LINE EXCEPT THE DOTTED LINES. SECTION 'Y' SHOULD BE FOLDED UNDER SECTION 'Z' THE TWO LINK PIECES SHOULD BE SLOTTED TOGETHER AND

FOLDED UNDER SECTION 'X' FINALLY, GLUE TOGETHER

Championship can begin, players using cardboard mailing tubes and ping pong balls.

Model railway landscape items Trees can be made from small well-branched twigs, decorated with pieces of tapioca, stuck on and painted green for leaves. Engine sheds, signal boxes and ticket offices can be cut from blocks of polystyrene (often used as packaging) and painted appropriately in emulsion or water colour paints.

For the football enthusiasts:

A football rattle in the form of a Dutch percussion instrument

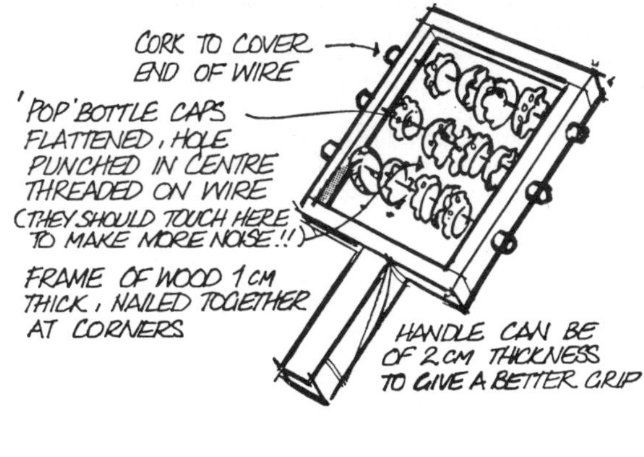

called a 'schelleraam'. It is made from wood, wire and 'pop' bottle-tops, and involves using a saw to cut out the wood after careful measuring, a drill to make holes to take the wires, and a hammer and nails.

A football string-bag carrier These carriers are reasonably easy to make, once the knack of netting has been acquired. This is something different for an individual boy to try, and as there is no mess involved he could continue at home. Bottle bags, and string shopping bags are good bazaar items. *(Net making for All* by Charles Holdgate, published by Mills & Boon, is one of the best books on the subject, borrow it from the Public Library and you will soon have a good understanding of the process.)

For Mum:

A tea-pot stand made of a plyboard base, with four small blocks stuck on the corners for legs, covered on top with a self-adhesive lino tile. If making several, cut the tiles up into shapes and create a mosaic pattern on top.

String picture A fairly thick ($\frac{1}{2}$ inch) base board is covered with felt or brushed nylon. Nails are knocked into the board with about half an inch left protruding, to form a geometric pattern or picture. A continuous string, or strong lurex thread, is then wound from nail to nail to form the pattern or picture. A page from a children's 'dot-to-dot' drawing book can be used as a guide for positioning the nails and can be torn away when all are in position.

Pewter work Boys who prove fairly dextrous should be able to produce a good standard of pewter work. Pendants, brooches and serviette rings can be made and decorated quite simply. More complicated designs can be used on the lids of jewellery boxes which, with the addition of a musical movement, can become a very special piece of work—a musical box.

Collage Try making a wall-frieze about 'International Scouting' or 'our District', or 'the Country Code'. Almost anything can be stuck on—pictures from magazines, small flags, food labels, stamps, coins, maps, paper plates, doileys, disposable cups, material, natural objects.

Artists Encourage individuals who may show an ability at sketching, painting or hand-writing, to contribute to your Pack Log-book, or to design a 'Thank-you' card, or a 'Get Well' card for a friend of the Pack.

Health and First Aid

Training aids

Books

* *Manual of First Aid,* published jointly by The British Red Cross Society, The St Andrew's Ambulance Association and the St John Ambulance Association. **Be sure to use the current edition, first aid treatment can change very rapidly.**

*† *The Scout Badge and the Scout Standard* by Steve Scholes (The Scout Association) for details of the Scout First Aid Kit.

† *Activities for Cub Scouts* (Gilwell Park)

Posters

Posters can also be obtained on various aspects of health, hygiene and first aid from such associations as: The General Dental Council, 37 Wimpole Street, London W1. Educational Productions Ltd., East Ardsley, Wakefield, Yorks

Who might help

Members of the local branch of the St John Ambulance Association, the British Red Cross or St Andrew's Ambulance Association
Local Scouters who have completed a recognised course run by one of the above
Local doctor, nurse or dentist

Planning

It must have been a Scouter who said 'Show me a mixture of noise and dirt and I'll show you a Cub Scout', and it is true that cleanliness is not a subject which interests many boys between 8 and 11 years old.
It is all the more important for leaders to devise imaginative activities to put over the subject of health in the Pack.
First aid has more appeal than hygiene, because in their world

of make believe boys may see themselves saving a life in some dramatic way. We must be careful to make them understand the limits of their ability. In most cases it is far more important that they should be able to run for help quickly and deliver a message correctly, than try to treat the patient. Imagine yourself lying with a broken leg after an accident, and ask how best you think Peter or David or John could help you in such a situation.

The first aid requirements of the Arrow badge are designed to make the Cub self-reliant and able to cope with the minor injuries which he might sustain himself, and the contents of the Cub Scout First Aid Kit enable him to deal with these small accidents, for which training has been given. The kit forms the basis of the Scout First Aid Kit, and as he progresses to the Troop the boy will add to his personal equipment as his knowledge is extended. Some Cub Scouts, of course, will wish to train for the First Aider badge and will add to their kit at that point, as they learn further facts and skills.

Example speaks louder than words, and it is pointless to talk about the need for strict cleanliness in first aid, and then offer boys very grubby materials with which to practise. Ask one of your Assistants to be responsible for keeping all first aid dressings in the practice kit in good condition. It goes without saying that the real First Aid Kit should never be used for training; it must always be ready for use in an emergency.

Putting it over

Health Bingo! Prepare a set of cards as illustrated. In order to make sure only one person wins, go through the cards and cross out two different pictures on each card, the aim being to get a complete line across. Distribute the cards to the Pack, together with some counters.

Problems are then put to the boys, who put a counter on the picture which they think represents the right answer:

'You use this to obtain help in an emergency'

'These foods are good for you'

'These enemies are floating around in the air to trap careless Cubs'

'These should be brushed for two minutes after every meal'

Go through the clues fairly quickly, and play only about two games. The winner receives a toothbrush! The Cubs enjoy playing 'Bingo' and it can be used sparingly as a means to an end, not an end in itself. It is useful on a coach journey, or a wet day in camp.

Feet Each Six makes a list of as many people as possible who rely on keeping their feet in good condition to be able to do their jobs: footballers, boxers, postmen, bus conductors, shop assistants, waitresses. Check off the answers, or have each Six name one of the occupations on their list in turn, and the others tick it off.
Teeth Dentists recommend that teeth be cleaned for two minutes at a time. Few people do take as long as this. On a Pack Holiday remove all watches and clocks from view and have a teeth-cleaning competition. Everyone starts together and stops when they think two minutes have passed. A tube of toothpaste is the reward for the one who guesses most accurately.
Acting A mime or a puppet play might be compiled about summoning adult help quickly.
Or a group of boys working for the Gold Arrow might enact a scene following instructions: the Cub Scout Instructor was stung by a wasp, and this made him jump and he missed his footing and fell, grazing his knee and elbow and cutting both hands. The rest of the Pack may watch them rendering first aid.
Yarn Often a story may be found in the newspapers about a real-life situation in which someone gave help at the scene of an accident. A discussion might follow as to what they needed in order to help, and if they did the right thing.

Singing Compose a song about the Health Rules.
A Quiz may be useful in revision, or in arousing fresh interest in a subject.
Two teams might compete in a quick-fire quiz, stating if a variety of accidents would result in a burn or a scald. The leader would suggest such accidents as a steaming kettle, an electric iron, a coal fire, a garden fire, a pan of vegetables being cooked, an open oven door, a gas ring, and so on.
Demonstration Invite a Patrol Leader to the Pack Meeting to demonstrate to the boys working for their Gold Arrow how to extinguish burning clothing.
Charts—Stings Find or draw two large pictures showing the difference between a wasp and a bee. A Cub might mount these on a chart, and write underneath instructions for treating insect bites and stings.
Nose bleed Another chart might be devised, showing the treatment for a nose-bleed.
Health rules One boy lies on his back on a very large sheet of paper, and the other Cubs draw his outline. Then fill in the features, and round the edge write the appropriate health rules: 'Brush teeth after every meal', 'Wash feet every day', 'Breathe through the nose', etc. Attach coloured strings from the health rules to the part of the anatomy to which they refer. This makes a striking wall chart.

Home Safety

Training aids

The Royal Society for the Prevention of Accidents (RoSPA), Cannon House, The Priory Queensway, Birmingham, B4 6BS—produces excellent material on all aspects of safety, much of it especially written for children. A comprehensive catalogue price list is available. Most of the material listed below is produced by them.

Books

My Home Safety Book—Workbook SE29
† *Activities for Cub Scouts* (Gilwell Park)

Cards

How clever are you with fireworks?—Hint card BMH31 (contains a quiz for children on firework safety)

Charts

Find the Dangers in Careless Cottage—HSP CP1 (10in x 15in)
Spot the Good Turns—HSP CP3 (10in x 15in)
Spot the Faults—HSP CP6 (10in x 15in)
Spot the Christmas Hazards—HSP CP7 (10in x 15in)
These charts are ideal for use with either an individual or a small group. They can be mounted on card or thin plywood and cut up to make jigsaws.
Fire Prevention—HSP 104-5 (20in x 30in)

Flannelgraph

Home Safety Flannelgraph—HS71—contains over 80 separate pieces.

Who might help

Local Accident Prevention Officer—contact local Police Station
The Fire Brigade
W.R.V.S. Emergency Service
The co-operation of each boy's parents will help to reinforce the training given

Planning

Activities promoting self-preservation should form part of a Cub Scout's training from his early days with the Pack. Boys of Cub Scout age are adventurous and, very often, oblivious of danger, and therefore vulnerable to accidents. Such activities should be included in the programme frequently.
Safety can, however, seem to be a very negative and dull subject to a small boy, a mere succession of 'Dont's'. Cub Scout leaders need to be positive-minded and arrange games and projects in which boys can enjoy playing an active part, and which will help to instil good habits. Accidents in the home increase in winter-time, so that is the season on which to focus attention on Home Safety.

Putting it over

Home safety trail
Prepare in advance a Home Safety Trail through your headquarters. The Cub Scouts pass along the trail without speaking to one another, and afterwards each Six prepares a list of faults which they spotted, e.g. toys lying on floor, aspirin

bottle left open on the table, frayed rug, matches within reach of small children, etc.

Make a collage or poster of dangers in the home This might include: broken glass, frayed flex, knives, medicines, unguarded fires, polythene bags, weed killers, hot ashes, cigarette ends, spilt grease, frost on outside steps.

Make a home safety 'notice board' Each boy makes a small chart showing how to get help in case of an emergency at his home, e.g. how to summon the fire brigade, the name, address and telephone number of the nearest doctor; the location and route to the nearest hospital which deals with accidents; the whereabouts of the nearest telephone. Cut-out-pictures could be used as symbols to give the chart more impact. Fasten a string through two holes on the top edge, so that it can be hung up at home.

Declare a 'home hazard spotting' week Each boy is asked to be on a special look-out for hazards that arise in his own home during the week. Such events as: 'Dad wound insulating tape round the splintered broom handle.' 'Dog's tail knocked matches on to floor from low table. Mum put them on top shelf.' He reports these to his Sixer together with any preventive measures that were taken. After Inspection the next week, each Sixer might read out the collected list.

Miming or play-acting Give each Six a card describing an incident to enact:

'All the family are returning home from work and school, and getting ready for the meal Mum is cooking, when the chip pan catches fire.'

'The telephone rings and while Mum goes to answer it, baby gets down from his chair and begins to play "houses" with the fire guard which is moveable.'

'Dad is quietly reading the newspaper, when grandma slips on the frayed rug and falls on to the paraffin stove.'

Afterwards the other Sixes discuss what was wrong and what would have prevented the accident or how they could have dealt with it.

Paper bag puppets Each boy makes a paper bag puppet, and the Cub Scouts working for their Gold Arrow organise the others in the production of a puppet play on a home-safety theme.

Have a Right or Wrong quiz The Cubs run to record their vote by making a mark on Right or Wrong sheets of paper, or putting a bean in an appropriate circle, in response to such statements as:

Never keep fireworks in your pocket. Right or Wrong?

The only poisonous British snake is the adder or viper. Right or Wrong?

Always pull out an electric plug by tugging the wire. Right or Wrong?

Wall frieze All the Pack might help to produce a large wall frieze in bright colours, to include the 'Firework Code'. Try and arrange to have it displayed in a local shop window the week before Bonfire Night.

Demonstration that fire needs air Place a jam-jar over a lighted candle. The flame will quickly go out as the oxygen is used up. This proves the importance of shutting all doors and windows if there is a fire in the house.

Yarns

— on summoning help.
— on knowing the right action to take in an emergency.
— about the Bonfire Party that was saved from being a disaster by one boy who persuaded the others to handle fireworks correctly.
— about the careless householder.

Parents' Evening Use Home Safety as a theme for a parents' evening, to inform them about the tests and gain their co-operation. Include a competition, for example the Home Safety Trail in which the parents can compete against the Cubs.

International Scouting

Training aids

Books

† *Hello World* (The World Scout Bureau)—ideas for programmes and activities. Available from Gilwell Park

- †* *The Commonwealth Cub Scout Book* by Falcon Travis (Brockhampton Press)
- * *Cubs International Quiz Book 1* by John Sweet (John Goodchild)
- †* *International Cub Scout Book* (World International Publishing Limited)

Who might help

Venture Scouts who have been to a Jamboree
A Scouter from overseas
Assistant County Commissioner (International)

Planning

If a British Cub Scout attended a Pack Meeting abroad, he would probably feel much more at home if he found boys doing the same sort of activities as his own Pack enjoys, even though the language might not be English. But obviously the history or culture or climate of other countries has often led to the introduction of activities in their programmes which are not so common in ours. Yet many of these activities can be carried out in this country, and Cub Scouts would enjoy actually 'doing' and not just 'hearing' about Scouting overseas.

Putting it over

United States of America

Early settlers in America had to pioneer a way into unknown territory. They were able to carry very little equipment, but with a few basic tools they were skilled enough to build themselves houses and make furniture. Perhaps it is because of this tradition that Cub Scouts in the U.S.A. enjoy 'whittling'—that is making something using a pocket-knife. One of their badge requirements is:

(1) Show that you know how to take care of and use a pocket-knife.
(2) Know the rules for handling a knife.
(3) Make something with your penknife.

Their leaders reason that if parents have allowed a boy to have a penknife then he is old enough to learn how to use it properly and appreciate that a knife is not a toy but a useful tool.

Most British boys long for their first penknife and when they get it, they are apt to find that the only available wood is table tops, tree trunks or chair-legs. It is surely better for a boy to be encouraged to use a knife safely on a piece of spare wood than to experiment without supervision. Your Scout Leader or Group Scout Leader might be persuaded to come along and work with a few boys, helping them to appreciate how to treat their penknives.

Again from America come the following conservation requirements—which are just as relevant here:

> *'Make a list of the things that make our water and air dirty and less useful to us.'*
>
> *'List six ways to make your block or neighbourhood more beautiful. Talk with your Leader about which of the things you might do. Then do one of them.'*

Or from their Family Fun achievement:

> *'Make an indoor game and play it with your family.'*

Or their Kites project:

> *'Explain the safety rules for kite flying.'*
>
> *'Make and fly a two-stick kite.'*
>
> *'Make and fly a box kite.'*

Or their Machinery project:

> *'Name and describe the use of 10 different kinds of trucks, or construction equipment or farm machinery.'*
>
> *'Use a lever, a pulley, a wheel, and an axle. Tell how they can help you do the job.'*

Or their Indians project:

'Make an Indian weapon such as a tomahawk, spear, bow and arrow or an Indian shield.'

'Make an Indian costume, and a tom-tom.'

New Zealand

Just as Indians are part of the American history, so the Maori are an integral part of New Zealand culture. Many European

games were known to the Maori long ago. The game we know variously as Five Stones, Knucklebones or Snobs, played by throwing five small stones into the air and catching them in various ways, was called Koruru by the Maori and played to develop quickness of the hand and eye. Why not hold a Pack Koruru Championship—the three finalists to challenge the Patrol Leaders, or the Brownies?

They were also skilled at String Games—such as 'Cat's Cradle', 'Six Diamonds' and many others. String games are a pastime enjoyed by young and old alike the world over, the designs and patterns, made by stretching a cord between the hands, representing some object or incident in mythology. (See *String Games for Beginners* by Kathleen Haddon (W. Heffer & Sons Ltd, Cambridge)).

Another popular pastime in New Zealand was stick games in which players kneel opposite each other, tapping sticks to the ground before throwing them from one to another, to their own chanting. Young warriors practised the stick games to improve their dexterity, alertness and rhythm. These stick games are best taught by someone who is already skilled at them, but if there is no such person in your district, then you can obtain details of these and the other games mentioned in a book called *'Games and Dances of the Maori'*, a guide book for teachers which is available from New Zealand House, Haymarket, London S.W.1.

Apart from these activities, New Zealand Cub Scouts wanting

to earn their Maoritanga Badge have to make a simple flax mat, re-tell a legend, do a simple carving, and know some of the Maori names for places, plants, animals and food. These would not be easy for British Cubs, nor could they point out the Southern Cross—one of the constellations only visible in the Southern hemisphere, and an important one for New Zealand boys because it is depicted on their National Flag.

We can however turn cartwheels as a test of agility, as New Zealand Cubs do, also *'explore a creek, pond or beach on a Pack outing, and show an adult three things you have discovered.'*

Belgium

Nearer to home Cub Scouts in one of the Belgian Associations have great fun carrying out their agility tests which include:

walking across a beam 3 metres long and 12 cms. wide, placed at the height of a table, carrying a full glass of water;

practising 'the walk of Bagheera' (i.e. walking on all fours) for 30 metres;

roller skating;

walking on stilts.

They also have to play Kim's game, observing 12 articles for one minute, and then remembering 10 of them. Another requirement is to make a 'Turk's head' woggle—quite a challenge for a boy of Cub age; and how to make a square lashing and, with Akela's help, use this in constructing a camp gadget. When a boy reaches 10 years old, he is expected to train a new boy in one of the tests and show by his example what it means 'to be a Cub Scout'.

These are only a few ideas from other countries which might be included in meetings in this country; others such as ski-ing —a requirement in the Scandinavian countries—would not be so easy to carry out. But a little imagination can overcome most difficulties: long strips of cardboard tied to the feet give a realistic feeling of the awkwardness of moving about on skis, and can be used for fun in a relay game.

Other ideas to stress the international angle might include:

—teaching the Pack songs from other countries, e.g. Waltzing Matilda, Frère Jaques, The Great American Railway;

—having a party using foods from as many different countries as possible;

—having a foreign coins exhibition, finding the countries from which they come, deciding what boys in those countries might buy with the coins; ice-cream, a fur cap, a coconut.

Make a scrap book of your Pack to send to a Pack abroad. It might include: a photograph of each Six, a map of the area, drawings of places of interest, pictures of the local football team, details of schools the Cubs attend, wrappers from favourite bars of chocolate, postage stamps, coins, details of favourite games played, leaves of trees in the area. The addition of a few comics might be appreciated.

Exchange tapes with a Pack abroad.

Write a prayer for Cub Scouts in other countries.

If you have difficulty in making contact with a Pack in another country, write for the Programme Information Exchange No. 9 *'Launching the World Scout Link Scheme'* which gives full details and is available, free of charge, from the World Scout Bureau, Case Postale 78, 1211 Geneva 4, Switzerland.

The Jungle Background

Training aids

Books

* *The Jungle Book* by Rudyard Kipling (Macmillan & Co Ltd)
* *The Second Jungle Book* by Rudyard Kipling (Macmillan & Co Ltd)
* *All the Mowgli Stories* by Rudyard Kipling (Macmillan & Co Ltd)

Who might help

The Assistant District Commissioner (Cub Scouts)
The District Cub Scout Leader
Other Pack Scouters

Planning

To appreciate the use of the jungle stories as a background to Cub Scouting, one must have an understanding of the mind of a child, and particularly the importance of imagination. Fantasy is often much more real for a child than fact. It helps him to escape reality, or to modify it until he can accept it. The animals of the jungle stories will come alive for him and he will recognise and identify some of the characteristics: the wolf, who knows how to live in Society, an example of law-abiding intelligence; Baloo, a symbol of wisdom; Bagheera, agility and sagacity; Shere Khan as the bully, with a streak of cowardice; the Banderlog, as examples of shortsightedness, anarchy and disorder. This will help boys to evolve their own scale of values in an acceptable form, which is the basis of moral sense.

When Mowgli had learned all there was to learn in the jungle, he left it behind and took his place in the real world of men. The wise Akela in the Cub Scout Pack will recognise the moment when a boy is ready to leave the jungle behind and to break off that special relationship with Akela. He will increasingly become more realistic and capable, until he is ready for a different relationship with others of his own age, more independent of adults. This he will find in the Patrol System in the Troop.

We must recognise that the time a boy spends in the Pack as a journey between two given points in time. As he travels, he is constantly adjusting, developing, growing up. When he has out-grown his early interests and preoccupations, and has gained some security and independence, it is proof that we have achieved what we set out to do.

Rudyard Kipling's *Jungle Book* provided Cub Scouting with some of its ceremonies: the Grand Howl, the Investiture and acceptance into the Pack, and the Going-up Ceremony. On these occasions a certain ritual takes place, and this symbolism often has more effect than words. Taking part in such ceremonial makes a boy feel that he belongs to the Pack and is as capable as the others, and on this basis the Grand Howl becomes an acceptable way to begin and end meetings.

But if a boy does not know the stories then the meaning will be lost to him, and he will only be learning to accept a bit of nonsense without question.

Putting it over

Cub Scout Games published by The Scout Association, suggests several games based on the jungle stories.

Cut out large templates of the jungle animals in cardboard, and help younger boys to use them to cut out a set of animals for themselves from polystyrene tiles. They can be painted appropriately.

Have a competition for the new boys to look at pictures of the animals and name them correctly.

Some may enjoy trying to mould an animal in plasticine, or make cut-outs of the animals into finger puppets, or make a 'King's Ankus' in a handcraft session.

Include the story of 'The Spring Running', the week before a Going-up Ceremony.

The story of the 'Red Dog' or *'The Death of Shere Khan'* lend themselves well to being acted by a small group, preferably out-of-doors where the 'fighting' can take place on grass.

Several of the stories can be portrayed well by shadowgraph.

The story of 'Mowgli's entry into the Pack' could be put over in this way to new boys, by a group of older Cubs, who could make a tape recording of the story first. There is a lot of drama and excitement to be found in the stories, if they are well put over.

Knotting

Training aids

Books

* *A Dictionary of Knots*—No 27 in the Patrol Book Series—by Eric Franklin (The Scout Association)

*† *Your Book of Knots* by Percy Blandford (Faber and Faber)
* *String Games for Beginners* by Kathleen Haddon (W. Heffer and Sons Ltd)
† *Activities for Cub Scouts* (Gilwell Park)

Cards

Knots for Everybody—a pull-out card (The Girl Guides Association)

Who might help

Other leaders in the Group
Venture Scouts
Ranger Guides
Patrol Leaders

Planning

Some boys seem 'all fingers and thumbs' and take weeks to learn to do even the simplest reef knot, while others will prove very dextrous and enoy learning to tie and use far more knots than will be found in the Arrow Training Scheme.

Patience will be needed to help those who find knotting difficult, but there are one or two tips which will be found helpful. Try to involve the Cub Scout in some activity in which a knot is required—perhaps fastening the flag to the halyards, or securing a line on a kite. So the boy will learn how to make the knot only when he has seen the need for it, and not just to pass a test.

Check whether the boy is right-handed or left-handed, as this will probably affect his approach. You should be able to tie the knots both ways. Stand alongside the boy to demonstrate—if you stand in front of him he will get a mirror image. Use ropes of different colours if possible as this makes it easier to follow the different strands.

Make a habit of hanking all ropes after use. Maintain all ropes in good condition and deal with fraying ends immediately. It is important to set an example of caring for ropes properly as one day, perhaps when rock-climbing, someone's life may depend on the condition of a rope, as well as the use of the right knot. Ropes for use in the Pack should be of a suitable thickness for boys' hands and not too stiff. The right materials will make learning more easy.

Putting it over

Miming situations Issue each Six with the required materials and a card giving a situation which involves tying a knot: 'You are rowing in to the jetty and are about to tie up your boat to one of the mooring rings.' 'You are sending some books to a cousin for his birthday, by parcel post. Fasten them up securely.' 'Your fishing line was broken when it rubbed against a rock, tie the two ends together again.' 'On a Pack Holiday the cook has asked you to "invent" a washing line so that she can hang out the tea-towels.'

The Six decide what knot to use, and then mime the situation, demonstrating the knot. The other Sixes guess what the mime was about and decide whether the right knot was used. One of the leaders checks that the knot was correctly tied.

Experts Invite a rock-climber, a small-boat sailor, or a fisherman to come to the Pack and demonstrate some of the knots they use, explaining their importance.

Obtain some old short ends of a variety of ropes. Let the Cubs unravel them to see how they are made or 'laid'.

Go on a knot-spotting expedition to a place such as a harbour, or a camp site, where you are likely to see several knots in use.

Rescue the Sixers The Pack lines up in Six relay formation and each boy is given a piece of rope, some of them being of different thicknesses. The Sixer then goes to the other end of the room, leaving his piece of rope with the Six. On the word 'go' the last boy in the Six ties his piece of rope to the piece held by the boy in front of him, using either the reef knot or the sheet bend. This is checked by a leader before the next Cub joins his rope to the one in front of him, and so on down the line. When all ropes are tied together, the boy at the front throws a life-line to the Sixer who must tie the rope round himself, using a bowline. The rest of the Six can then haul him back to join the Six.

Challenge Knotting Give each Six a pile of small lengths of rope. On a given signal they begin tying as many pieces together as possible, using reef knots, before the whistle blows. Points for all correct knots.

Stretch a rope across the room. As a relay race the first boy in each Six picks up a piece of string, runs to the rope and ties the string on to it using a round turn and two half-hitches, then returns to his place, and the next boy runs and does the same. The Six with most pieces of string tied on to the rope by the time the whistle blows wins.

Challenge another local Pack to a blindfold knot-tying competition.

Challenge the Brownies to a life-line throwing competition.

Knotting in handcrafts

Learn how to do French knitting and make a useful article with it.

Learn how to net a football carrier string bag (see 'Handcrafts').

Learn how to plait.

Learn how to make a 'Turk's Head' woggle.

Join a piece of string with a reef knot to form a loop, and play a String Game—'Cat's Cradle', etc.

The Link Badge, The Founder and the History of the Movement

Training aids

Books

* *Cub Scouts—who they are and what they do* (Ladybird Books Ltd)

* *Scouts—who they are and what they do* (Ladybird Books Ltd)

† *Baden-Powell, the Two Lives of a Hero* by William Hillcourt with Olave, Lady Baden-Powell (Heinemann Ltd)

* *The Scout Badge and the Scout Standard* by Steve Scholes (The Scout Association)

*† *The Patrol Leader's Handbook* (The Scout Association)

Films

B.-P. Chief Scout of the World

Can be hired from: The Central Film Library, Government Building, Bromyard Avenue, Acton, London W3 7JB

Film Strips

*† *Cub Scouts—who they are and what they do*

*† *Scouts—who they are and what they do*

These are reproductions of the illustrations in the Ladybird books of the same name. They can be cut up and mounted to make a set of slides. Mounts are available from Scout Shops Ltd.

Pictures

* *The Founder, Lord Baden-Powell* Reproductions of David Jagger's portrait, sizes from 22in x 17½in down to postcard size.

Tape Cassettes

*† *The Story of Lord Baden-Powell* narrated by Michael Aspel (Small Talk) available through record shops

Who might help

District Scouters
Group Scout Leader and Scout Leader
Venture Scouts and Patrol Leaders
Other Pack Scouters

Planning

Although the Cub Scouts working for the Link Badge will wish to make some specific projects about the Founder and the History of the Movement, such activities are of interest to all boys in the Pack. Make the most of opportunities to build up the Cubs' knowledge of the Movement throughout his time in the Pack. They might be interested to know that Lord Baden-Powell coined the term 'Boy Scouts' in 1908 when he founded the world-wide movement. The word 'Scout' comes from a Latin word 'auscultare' meaning 'to listen with hidden ear' or 'to harken'. An Old French word 'escouter' meant 'to eavesdrop' or 'to spy'. In 15th century England, soldiers sent ahead of an Army to spy on the enemy were called scouts.

Putting it over

Invite the District Commissioner to talk to the Pack about how Scouting began.

If the Group has been in existence for some time, ask the Group Scout Leader to show pictures and talk about the early days of the Group.

Plan a Special Pack Meeting using 'The Life of B.-P.' as the theme. Play excerpts from the tape *'The Story of Lord Baden-Powell'* to set the scene.

Invite a neighbouring Pack to join your Pack to celebrate the Founder's birthday on February 22nd, or join with the Brownies on this day which they celebrate as 'Thinking Day'.

Invite the Sixers from two or three neighbouring Packs to join with your Pack, and hire a film of the most recent Jamboree to show them.

Take the Pack to visit the Troop in camp Arrange for each Patrol to adopt a Six for the day.

Ask a Patrol Leader to talk to the Pack about the adventures of summer camp.

Plan a Pack expedition to B.-P. House in London; or to Gilwell Park, the International Training Centre for leaders, and camping grounds for boys; or *Brownsea Island,* the scene of that famous first camp.

Invite a Venture Scout, who has been Scouting abroad, to show the Pack some of his souvenirs and colour slides.

On your next Cub Camp or Pack Holiday arrange a joint meeting with another Pack in that area.

Consider the possibility of inviting a Pack from a different environment to have a Pack Holiday in your headquarters, if it is suitable. Ask the older boys to prepare a guide-book of the area and send it to them beforehand.

Invite the Patrol Leaders to meet the Scouters of the Group, perhaps to have coffee one evening, and discuss the Link Badge and how it is operating in your Group.

Hold a Parents' evening designed to tell some of the History of the Movement and to inform parents about Scouting.

Mapping

Training aids

Books

- * *Understanding Maps* (Ladybird Books Ltd)
- † *The Map that Came to Life* by Deverson (Oxford University Press)

* *Know the Game—Map Reading* (Educational Productions Ltd)

† *Map and Compass Way: Orienteering* by John Disley (Blond Educational)

In the Street I-Spy Series (Model and Allied Publications Ltd)

Signs and Symbols I-Spy Series (Model and Allied Publications Ltd)

On the Road I-Spy Series (Model and Allied Publications Ltd)

On a Car Journey I-Spy Series (Model and Allied Publications Ltd)

Charts

Map Reading—SP15—SCOUTING Magazine Training chart. Available from the Editorial Department of Headquarters

Who might help

Group Scout Leader and Scout Leader
Venture Scouts

Planning

Like compass work, learning to use a map should be done out-of-doors if it is to have any meaning to a Cub Scout, although some preparatory work can be done indoors, such as learning the map symbols.

It is helpful if you can take a few boys at a time to sit on a high hill, or to a good vantage point, like a church tower or other tall building, then they can observe various features and locate them on the map. They will come to appreciate that the map is a kind of 'bird's eye view' of the ground.

A look at the same area of maps of different scales will help them to see the usefulness of each type—large scale maps when walking, smaller scale when travelling long distances in a car.

An appreciation of contour lines is also needed but check that the Cubs have not already learnt about them at school. Making a model hill from plaster of paris on a foundation of chicken wire gives a realistic impression, particularly if the model can be of a local hill which can later be climbed.

Again like compass work, using a map represents real adventure to the Cub Scout and forms the basis of much of his Scout training. Even as a Cub, map-reading will be a useful asset on many family outings and Pack Expeditions.

Putting it over

Ideas to use indoors in preparation for going out-of-doors.

Map symbol cards On a set of postcards draw the mapping symbols. Lay them out in a row across one end of the room. In front of each Six, on smaller cards write the names of the various symbols. Each boy in turn picks up a name and tries to place it on the right symbol.

True or false Distribute the cards used in the game above—one to each boy. Each in turn holds up his card showing the symbol and calls out the name of a symbol. This can either be the right name or the name of a different one. The other Cubs are expected to mark a card 'true' or 'false' as they think fit.

Map sign bingo Play as 'Health Bingo' but substitute map symbols on the cards.

Matching pairs Collect from magazines or papers some photographs of churches, telephone kiosks, main roads, country lanes, river bridges, electricity supply power lines, orchards, marsh land, etc. For each photograph draw on a separate card the map symbol used. Cub Scouts try and pair up the photographs with the correct symbols.

Activities out-of-doors

'Bring a map to life' Before an expedition to an area unknown to the Pack, let the older boys study a map of the route to be taken and write down, in order, what they think they will see on the way. Check this during the trip, and let them see how accurate they were, and what they overlooked.

Going on a Pack Holiday Let a group of boys who don't know the area act as the 'planning team'. From the map they can work out the nearest place to post their letters home, whether the church has a tower or a spire, the road numbers that lead to the site, the nearest farm, any items of historical interest, and so on. Older boys, with some knowledge of contours, might estimate whether they will be able to see certain features from the site or whether other buildings or land will block the view. The boys have great fun checking whether they were right and will learn by discovery why some features were different from what they expected.

Carry out a 'signpost' survey Check how many different sign posts can be found near your headquarters. It will be of interest to the Cubs to know that the old type of stone mile-stones were placed so that people on foot could read them, and the wooden 'finger-posts' were at a height ideal for travellers on horse-back; and then to deduce why the metal road-signs used today are so placed, and why the lettering is so large on motorway signs.

Weather cocks on churches: the cock is said to be used as a reminder of Peter's denial of Christ. What other symbols are used on weather vanes, and why?
Sheep-counting gates, kissing gates—any other kinds?
Large stone balls on top of gate posts which are said to be relics from barbarian days when victors decorated their gateways with the heads of the vanquished.
'Downs'—why not 'ups'? Encampments and homesteads of ancient Britons built on high hills were called 'downs' by the inhabitants and the name has persisted; it has nothing to do with the lie of the land. The Saxons called their dwelling places 'hams' or 'burghs' or 'tuns' and these names can still be found in our present-day place names. What is the origin of your town's name?
Bench-marks Heights above sea-level are recorded by Bench Marks. These signs consist of a broad-arrow with a cross-piece on top, and are usually cut into corners of solidly built buildings: churches, stone walls, or on bridges, or whatever is likely to remain in position over a long period of time. Government surveyors do this work, to record the heights of certain places above sea-level. The official sea-level of Great Britain is taken as the mean level of the sea at Liverpool. The cross piece along the top is the 'bench' or ledge from which the exact height has been measured. The broad arrow dates from the 17th century when a man called Sidney was Master of the Ordnance and used his personal badge to mark the stones for which he was responsible. This same arrow was used to mark W.D. property and on the old time convicts' clothes, and the Crown department have continued to use this relic from the past.

On a large scale map of the area note the bench marks, then visit those spots and find the signs. It should be possible to establish which is the highest spot near your headquarters and which the lowest.

Special finds Encourage the Cubs to keep their eyes open for special finds in their own locality and try to discover the history behind them. Each discovery may lead to further questions: Market crosses were once 'preaching crosses'. Are there crosses of any other kind in the district?

A lychgate: a place where coffins rested before being taken into church. When there were no motor cars coffins might have been carried a long way. The word comes from the German 'leiche', meaning corpse. What other interesting features can be found around the church?

Dew ponds These saucer-shaped ponds can be found on the chalk downs from Sussex to the Marlborough and Wiltshire Hills. Chalk and flint were rammed down hard, then a layer of straw or reeds was added, finally a lining of clay. On a hot day, the ground around the pond is warmed but the heat cannot reach the clay because of the non-conducting layer of straw. When night falls, the cooler clay attracts more moisture from the atmosphere, counter-acting evaporation even on the hottest day, so there was always water available for the animals to drink. Other examples of how people of long ago used simple scientific facts to help them in their work can also be found.

'I-Spy' discoveries Work out your own list of questions based on the 'I-Spy' series of books, to help the Pack discover the interesting features of the area, and draw a pictorial map to illustrate your finds.

Nature and Conservation

Training aids

There are innumerable books on all aspects of nature and conservation. The *I-Spy* series and the *Ladybird* books are among the cheaper ones and are excellent for Cub Scouts. Comprehensive guides such as *On the Seashore* (I-Spy Series) or *What to look for in Spring* (Ladybird Books Ltd) are particularly useful on Pack expeditions.

Books

† *Fun with Ecology* by Geoffrey Watson (Kaye and Ward)
† *Project Earth* by Graham Searle (Wolfe Publishing Ltd)
Something to do by Septima (Penguin Books) available in paperback—full of good ideas for each month of the year including a special 'out-of-doors' section; what to look for in the countryside; games to play, e.g. 'conkers'; gardening; pets; poetry.
The series of books on conservation produced by the World Scout Bureau give ideas for Pack and Troop projects and ideas.
† *Activities for Cub Scouts* (Gilwell Park)

Sound recordings

There is an increasing number of records and tapes coming onto the market; some are coupled with colour slides, for example:
Birds of the Countryside Midland Sound Recording MID BRD 6A/B

Magnifiers

S 3D Nature Viewers, the magnifying tubes, are easy for Cub Scouts to use. Available from the Visual Aids Centre, 78 High Holborn, London WC1 6NB.

Who might help

Local Vet.
Camp Warden
Other Pack Scouters
Friends whose hobby is bird-watching or who take a keen interest in other aspects of nature study

Council for Nature, 41 Queen's Gate, London SW7
R.S.P.C.A., 105 Jermyn Street, London SW1
Forestry Commission, 25 Savile Row, London W1
Keep Britain Tidy Group, Bostel House, 37 West Street, Brighton BN1 2RE.
The Royal Society for the Protection of Birds, The Lodge, Sandy, Beds, SG19 2DL

Planning

This is one of the Arrow Activity areas in which rural Packs score over those who meet in cities or suburban areas. Country boys seem to know (long before they reach Cub age) just where the best blackberries can be found, where birds are most likely to nest, where the first pussy willow of the season can be found and many other snippets of local information.
For such Cub Scouts the leader's job is to find a fresh aspect of a nature project in which the boys can become really involved. Many conservation activities will appeal to them but make sure that any project you undertake is not being currently carried out at school.
Boys who live in built-up areas, on the other hand, may be very unfamiliar with country matters. It will be necessary to explain the Country Code to them before setting out on an expedition, as they will probably not know how to behave in strange conditions. Apart from enjoying the day out they will be much impressed with the smallest evidence of animal life. They may come to realise that although they may not be able to do very much about saving the rarer species of big game in Africa, they can help to preserve wild life in Britain.
Leaders of such Packs will need to make greater efforts to get boys into the countryside, arranging transport, packed meals and adequate adult help. While local parks will provide some trees and flowers for study, it is well worth while taking the extra trouble to plan outings into the country from time to time.
If you choose to visit a nature trail or nature reserve, it is wise to take only a few boys at a time. A whole Pack together cannot help creating noise and movement and this will frighten off the birds and animals, and will spoil the day both for you and for any members of the public who may be visiting the reserve on the same day.

Putting it over

Trees A tree chart might be kept by each Six, to include a bark rubbing, a leaf print, a record of the height and spread of the tree, a picture of things that are made from the wood and any other items of interest they discover.

Measuring the spread of a tree combines a nature project and

the use of a compass. One member of a Six, using a compass, directs another Cub along each of the eight compass points in turn, until he is immediately beneath the outermost twigs of a big tree. The Cub counts aloud the number of paces he takes, while a third boy records the result. This may be marked on a paper on which a number of concentric rings have been drawn, each ring representing one pace with the trunk at the centre point. By joining the points together a rough sketch may be made of the spread of the tree, from which it might be possible to deduce the direction of the prevailing wind, or any other trees or buildings which block out the light.

Animal life may be observed on a ramble in the country, or may need to be pointed out before the Cubs can appreciate the evidence of such clues as nuts nibbled by field mice, sheep's wool on a barbed wire fence, droppings near a rabbit burrow. City-born boys will be thrilled to find such things as a bird's nest, a squirrel burying nuts, frog-spawn in a pond, or counting the rings of a felled tree to ascertain its age.

Boys who have pets could be asked to tell the rest of the Pack about them. Suggest some activities for them to do, to add interest to their talk: make a plaster cast of the pet's footprint or a sketch of the animal sleeping, or a list of what it likes to eat and how much it eats each day. It might even be possible for some pets to be brought along to one Pack Meeting and the local Vet. be persuaded to talk to the boys about the care of animals.

Birds Cubs will find it interesting to collect an old bird's nest in the autumn and discover what it is made of by dissecting it. The nest may be pulled apart and the various types of material separated, counted and measured. It is important to stress that nests should only be collected in autumn, never in spring or summer even if they appear to be deserted, as there is a possibility that they may still be in use.

Nesting boxes Perhaps your Group could make some nesting boxes and erect them at your local camp site, or in the grounds of an elderly people's home as a good turn.

Bird Puddings In hard weather the whole Pack can make 'puddings' for the birds, by melting some fat such as dripping and mixing into it cornflakes, seeds, nuts, currants, berries and bacon rind scraps. If a string is inserted before it sets, it can be hung up from a branch.

Bird tables might be made during handcraft sessions, especially by the older boys, who may like to erect them in their own gardens. Keep a chart of all the birds spotted during a two or three month period. Even in a busy city street or noisy estate a bird-table will usually attract some birds and prove a source of interest and delight.

Pond-dipping can be great fun at any age. A net can easily be made from a garden cane, an old nylon stocking and a piece of stiff wire. Fish, snails, water-beetles, frog or toad spawn and all sorts of wonderful things may be collected temporarily in a large jar until identified, and then tipped back into the pond.

Older boys might like to make a transect of the pond, measuring the depth at intervals and marking this on a chart to show the curve of the bottom of the pond. The plants growing in the water, and the trees and plants on the water's edge, can all be shown as they appear along the line of the transect. Others could make a plan of the surface of the pond and mark the features on it.

Just in case someone falls in, it would be wise to take some spare clothing along.

Seashore Those who live on the coast, or Packs who visit the seashore on a Pack expedition or Pack Holiday, will find plenty to interest them.

Shells can be collected, mounted and named. A number of matchbox drawers stuck into a large chocolate box give plenty of compartments in which to keep them.

Seaweed makes an unusual collection. Different varieties can be collected in a polythene bag and floated in a bowl of water before they dry out. When arranged in an attractive pattern, a postcard can be slid underneath and slowly lifted from the water. Most types of seaweed will be found to adhere to the card without the need of extra glue.

Easter eggs If the empty shells of soft-boiled eggs are kept and filled with earth, a pea or bean can be planted in them in spring to sprout in time for Easter.

Nature collections Individual boys may wish to make a specialised collection and these possibilities are almost endless: feathers, fossils, fungi (under guidance), autumn fruits, grasses, or animal tracks. Or they may develop an interest in insects or butterflies and any of these could become suitable projects at the Gold Arrow stage.

Here are some ideas for conservation projects suitable for Cub Scouts, and there are lots more under the section on the Country Code.

Clean up the surroundings of your headquarters and plant a garden.

Adopt a pond, clear out the debris, and get expert advice on how to maintain and improve it.

Visit a Zoo. Arrange for someone to explain to the Pack the role of zoos in saving rare animals from extinction.

Ask if you can turn a neglected churchyard or garden of an Elderly People's Home into a nature reserve, by planting bushes with berries which attract birds; or buddleia bushes which attract butterflies.

Carry out a survey in your area for evidence of ways in which man has damaged nature—perhaps quarries or old bomb-sites; and ways in which man has improved nature—planting gardens, reinstating coal-tips.

Co-operate with other local conservation agencies on a project to improve your locality.

Take out a group membership subscription to World Wildlife Youth Service or the Young Ornithologists' Club of the Royal Society for the Protection of Birds and benefit from the ideas in their magazines for projects, surveys, expeditions and holiday courses for children.
Persuade the Venture Scout Unit or a Brownie Guide Pack to join you in carrying out a project.
Have a conservation theme at your next camp, and co-operate with the Camp Warden on setting up a nature trail or conservation corner on the site.
Find out what Cub Scouts in other countries are doing to gain the World Conservation Badge, and tell them about your activities.

Photography

Training aids

Books

- *How it works—The Camera* (Ladybird Books Ltd)
- *Light, mirrors and lenses* (Ladybird Books Ltd)
- *Know the Game—Photography* (Educational Productions Ltd)

Leaflets

Kodak occasionally produce leaflets about photography suitable for children, some are available free of charge—write for details to: Kodak Ltd., Sales-Service Library, Victoria Road, Ruislip, Middlesex.

Who might help

A parent, friend, Venture Scout, District Scout Fellowship Member, or Scouter whose hobby is photography.
Local retailer of photographic equipment.
Local Camera Club.
(Amateur photographers often get carried away by their enthusiasm, so remember that very careful briefing is required if they are to retain the interest of small boys.)

Planning

This is another activity with particular appeal to older boys, and

may well be the start of a lifetime's hobby for some Cub Scouts.
Obviously it is a more expensive activity than most, and so it is better reserved for small groups of interested boys. This also makes it easier to train boys to handle photographic material with care.
If you can catch the moment when a boy has been given a camera, perhaps as a birthday present, he will be particularly keen to become involved in a photographic project. All the better of course if that project is a really important one, such as being the 'official photographer' of an expedition or Pack Holiday, when the pictures are needed for the Pack log-book.

Putting it over

If you have the opportunity to use a Polaroid camera, the Cubs will enjoy the instant results it gives. Encourage the boys

to discuss and decide on a theme and then concentrate on the treatment of the subject matter: long distance and close-up shots, action photographs, profiles and unusual angles. Some possible themes might be:—
'Our Pack'—for sending to a Pack abroad in an international link-up.
'The Grand Howl' in easy stages, for showing to new boys.
'Our Pets'—might prove more testing!
A pinhole camera might intrigue those boys who always like to know how everything works. (Details in Ladybird book—*How it works—The Camera.)*
A Photographic Chart is a useful home-made aid. Pictures may be cut out of a magazine, trimmed as required and mounted on large sheets of paper. One picture might have the heads cut off, another the feet, one might be blurred to show what happens

if the camera is not held steady, and one completely black square where a hand had been held in front of the lens!

Photograms This is an intriguing activity, suitable for a small group. Although not directly connected with the Photographer's badge, it does help boys to understand the first steps in developing and printing. A photogram is a shadow print, or contact print, producing a photographic image without the use of a camera or film. The leader must of course learn the technique before attempting to put it over.

Promise and Law

Training aids

Books

* *Pack Prayers* by Marion Treading (The Congregational Scout Fellowship)

*† *Scout Prayers* (The Scout Association)

* *Prayers for Catholics in Scouting* compiled by John Reynolds (The Catholic Scout Advisory Council)

Please God . . . by Beryl Bye and Joyce Badrocks (The Church Pastoral Aid Society)

Christ, the Light of the World by Sheila Mays (The Highway Press)

Let's talk to God by Zinnia Bryan (The Scripture Union)

† *Words for Worship* by Christopher Campling and Michael Davis (Edward Arnold)

The Bible There are many excellent children's editions which are ideal for Pack use.

† *Activities for Cub Scouts* (Gilwell Park)

Cards

* *The Cub Scout Promise and Law Card*—a pocket reminder, 2¼in x 3½in covered in permanent plastic.

Who might help

Group Scout Leader
Scout Leader
Assistant District Commissioner (Cub Scouts) or
District Cub Scout Leader
District Commissioner
Other Pack Scouters
Local clergy and other church workers

Planning

The Promise and Law is an Activity area just as much as handcrafts or firelighting, and as leaders we must seek practical ways to include it in our Pack Meetings. We must be careful not to put it in a special box to be taken out and dusted only on church parades, nor must we glibly say that it underlies all we do and so avoid doing anything in particular about it.
An acceptance of the Scout Promise and Law as adults is necessary before we can interpret it to boys, and it should be discussed occasionally on an adult level by the Pack Scouter Team, or at a Group Scouters' Meeting, or privately with the Assistant District Commissioner or anyone else who can help us to further our own understanding of the implications.
A boy needs opportunity for expansion spiritually, morally and socially, just as much as he needs opportunities for physical development and we should aim to provide such opportunities and challenges.

Putting it over

Projects on the Promise and Law
'Promise-Keepers' might be the name of this project. Two boys working together draw an outline of your headquarters on a large sheet of paper or draw a large Scout Badge. They then begin to collect the autographs of all the people they

know who have made the Promise. The Cub Scouts, Scouts and Venture Scouts are obviously the easy signatures to collect, together with the Scouters of the Group. A letter may need to be sent to the Assistant District Commissioner and District Commissioner asking for their signatures. What about members of the Group Council, teachers at school, parents and grandparents who have been in the Movement? Cub Scouts are sure to collect a great deal of other information during the course of the project. Eventually the paper full of signatures can be hung on the wall, and when new boys are invested they can be invited to add their names.

Different ways of serving the Queen and Country
Over the period of a month, build up a wall frieze of pictures of great men and women who in the past or at the present time have tried their best to do their duty to Queen and Country. Well known soldiers or explorers may easily come to

mind, but include people such as our one-time Chief Scout, Lord Maclean, the Lord Chamberlain, and some local Queen's Scouts who might be known to the Pack. Discuss the different ways of serving the Queen, and all that she stands for—not all are spectacular but some are well within the capabilities of Cub Scouts, such as keeping the laws of the land by not dropping litter, crossing the road in the proper manner, and respecting the flag.

Cub Scout Personal Log-book Help each boy to make a log-book before he is invested and write in it the Cub Scout Promise and Law, and underneath 'This is the Promise I have made today'. After his investiture he can sign the book and put the date. Details of badges he has gained, expeditions, or a Pack Holiday can be added during his time with the Pack. Boys will usually treasure their log-book after they go up into the Troop as a memento of their days as a Cub Scout.

7-day challenge cards These are very popular with Cub Scouts as they are clear and specific and achievements can be marked off. Various challenges may be devised as the boy's understanding of the Promise and Law develops. Two such Promise and Law 7-day challenge cards might read:

For a younger Cub Scout:

Monday	*'A Cub Scout always does his best—'* Keep room and personal belongings tidy.
Tuesday	*'He thinks of others before himself—'* Spend pocket money on someone who is ill (a Get Well card, book, etc.).
Wednesday	*'He does a good turn every day—'* Do something for Mum, Dad, brother, sister, grandparents, friends and neighbours.
Thursday	*'I promise that I will do my best—'* Do something difficult or something that you normally dislike doing.
Friday	*'Do my duty to God'—* Spend a few minutes longer today in prayer. Thank God for health and strength and Cub Scouting.
Saturday	*'Do my duty to the Queen—'* Keep the Queen's laws today: pick up any litter you may see lying about.
Sunday	*'Helps other people—'* Go out of your way today to help other people—in church—in the street—in the home.

For an older Cub Scout:

Monday	*'A Cub Scout always does his best—'* Have another try at something you have found hard to do and given up—perhaps swimming, arithmetic, keeping your bicycle clean, finding a way to keep your toys and books tidy.
Tuesday	*'He thinks of others before himself—'* Take a 'back-seat' today—play the games your friends choose to play, give other members of the family first choice of television programmes without arguing, make your own bed—don't leave it for Mum to do.

Wednesday	*'He does a good turn every day—'* Do something for someone you find hard to like, or for someone you haven't helped before.
Thursday	*'I promise that I will do my best—'* Explain (to a younger boy) what being a Cub Scout means. Check that you have carried out any promises you have made.
Friday	*'Do my duty to God—'* Thank God today for all the things you enjoy, and ask for His blessing on people you know who are less fortunate than yourself.
Saturday	*'Do my duty to the Queen—'* Give a lead to younger boys when crossing the road, show that you respect the Highway Code.
Sunday	*'Help other people'—* Use one of the skills of your Arrow Badge Training to help someone—take Mum and Dad a cup of tea in bed, clean the family's shoes, or offer to do a job at church—tidying bookshelves.

Some of the boys working on 'Flags and Countries' may have found that the different colours used in flags of various nations have certain meanings, depending on the climate ideology or history of the country; for example, white usually symbolises peace, and green agriculture. In the Christian church, the different colours used for vestments and furnishings also have meanings—white for purity, red for fire, black for mourning. In the ages when few people could read, the colourful stained glass windows in churches were used to tell a story. On our Church Parades there is often a 'Colour Party' carrying and escorting the flag. Cubs should be encouraged to question why this has become a custom, and what it signifies to those who are watching.

'To help other people at all times.' This is quite a tall order! Nor is it an easy subject to explain to Cubs, or to put over in a practical or attractive way. Probably yarns are the best means of showing instances of people who are unselfish, who go to help when they might prefer not to get involved, who are sympathetic and observant in spotting the needs of others, and have the skill to help.

Suggest that the boys look at the skills of the various Arrow requirements, and decide how they could use them to help others. Then start them thinking about the people who are pledged to help others at all times: Firemen, doctors and nurses, life-boatmen, mountain rescue teams, policemen, 'Samaritans', and so on. What skills do they have to have? Are any of them the same skills as those in Scouting? What about the risk involved to the rescuers? Why do many people help others on a voluntary basis?

Values
Cub Scouts about to go up to the Troop should be helped to think about the meaning of the Scout Law. They should be capable of debating aided by Akela, such matters as the true value of fast cars, boats, money: all the expensive things they would like to have when they are grown up, and then consider the value of the fast car after a road accident, in which a child lost a leg; the use of money if you were lost in a desert or up in space. Are 'values' dependent on the society within which we live? Are the values expressed in the Scout Law more important than luxury goods? Would they always have the same value at all times in all places?
The boys may then be more likely to remember a story or an incident, or to appreciate a yarn in which such relative values play a part.

Prayers
Experiment with the idea of having a postbox at your Pack Meeting in which the Cubs can post their requests for things to include in Pack prayers: 'Thank you, God, for . . .' or 'Please God . . . ." being the usual format.
Build up a Pack Prayer Book by encouraging each Six to write a prayer on a theme of their own choice and find a picture to illustrate their prayer. Stick the picture on one side of the page and the prayer on the other. Use the book frequently, and add to it from time to time.
Ask one Cub to repeat the Cub Scout Law occasionally before prayers, as a reminder to all the Pack.
Beware of Pack Meeting prayers becoming a meaningless ritual—an element of surprise is needed here just as much as in other activities. Let two or three boys arrange a suitable display to form a focal point for prayers—it isn't always necessary to stand with eyes closed. A display of handcrafts made by the Pack, a football and a pair of boots, a nature collection, a picture of B.-P., or the Queen or of Cub Scouts in other countries, could all be used if appropriate to specific prayers. A tape recording of bird song, or traffic sounds, or a reading from one of B.-P.'s books might be used to catch attention and lead into prayers.

A shadowgraph play of one of the parables, or a serious mime will give added impact.
On an expedition some could try and collect some of the flowers and plants mentioned in the Bible. The Ladybird book on this subject will help.
Discuss Pack Prayers at the Sixers' Council, listen to their suggestions and try to implement them.

Road safety

Training aids

The Royal Society for the Prevention of Accidents, Saftey Education Division, Cannon House, The Priory Queensway, Birmingham, B4 6BS, produces an excellent range of material, much of it particularly aimed at children. Most of the following items are theirs.

Books

My Road Safety Book—SE26—ages 7-11
My Second Road Safety Book—SE28—ages 8-12
The Cyclist's Safety Book—SE31—ages 9-13
Crossing the Road (An AA-RoSPA joint production)
The Highway Code (HMSO) essential reading for everyone
† *Activities for Cub Scouts* (Gilwell Park)

Charts

This Cycle is Unsafe!—SEP/J 195-6—Quiz picture
Keep away from farm vehicles—SEP/J 196-6—useful in rural Packs
If you see young children trying to cross the road, help them—SEP/J 191-6
The Green Cross Code—SEP/J 189-5

Films

Enquiries should be made to RoSPA, Film Library, 22 Soho Square, London W1V 5FJ (Tel 01-437 7991) quoting the age range of the audience.

Magazines

Safety Education A magazine produced each school term 'for everyone concerned with accident prevention'. Provides up-to-date information and programme ideas.

Leaflets

Walking on Country Roads—SE35
The Green Cross Code—SE33

Who might help

The Royal Society for the Prevention of Accidents, for resource material
Local Accident Prevention Officer—contact through local Police Station

Planning

When you look at the statistics—39,000 children involved in road accidents every year—it makes you marvel that any child survives. It is probable that 1 in every 20 children will be involved in an accident before he is 15, and the accident rate is particularly bad in the 5-9 year age range. Every Pack in the country must therefore be concerned in training Cub Scouts in matters of road safety. Don't leave it too late and then say **'If only . . .'**

The list of circumstances of fatal road accidents to children under 15 in Great Britain in one year showed that the greatest single cause was 'running into the road'.
It is worth checking your own habits, as responsible leaders,

by asking such questions as: Do you turn your Pack out in an excitable state at the end of the meeting, or do you conclude with a yarn or a few quiet songs? Does an adult see them across the road if you meet near a busy street? Do you always set a good example yourself, or do you dash across the road between moving vehicles and ignore the Zebra crossing? Do you praise a boy for practising safe road behaviour, or only criticise them for doing silly things? And which is less likely to have the desired effect?

There is never a 'wrong' time for including road safety in the programme, it should be a frequently recurring topic, though in different guises, to attract and maintain interest.

Putting it over

Encourage the Cubs to help with some positive project, such as:

'Black spots' and 'safety zones' Make a list of 'black spots' in the area around your headquarters, mark them on a large scale map. Then work out the best places to cross the road, for every boy in the Pack, as he walks from his home to headquarters, and mark these on the map. Mark too the places where it is safe to play.

Stop Watch With a stop watch, time how long it takes a boy to cross the road on the Zebra crossing. Then check how far a car being driven at average speed can travel in the same time. Work out how much clearance is required before stepping out on to the road.

Road Surveys Count the number of cars which pass in a quarter of an hour, and note how many of the drivers were wearing seat belts; how many were carrying children, and note if the children were sitting in the recommended safe place for them—the back seat.

Traffic Lights Make a poster or a moving training aid to show the order in which traffic lights change colour.

Invent a 'yell' about the Highway Code and get the Sixers to teach it to the Pack. Or run this as an inter-Six Competition.

Observation One boy takes an adult for a walk, preferably through a busy area. Another couple follow behind and note any errors made. They reverse positions on the way back.

'How far can you be seen?' Chart Check the luminosity of various types of clothing in the dark and make a graph of the findings, showing at what distance the following are visible:

a white sweater
reflective arm-bands
black wellingtons

Cub Scout uniform
faces and hands

Science

Training aids

Books

* *Levers, Pulleys and Engines* (Ladybird Books Ltd)
* *Magnets, Bulbs and Batteries* (Ladybird Books Ltd)
* *Air, Wind and Flight* (Ladybird Books Ltd)
* *Light, Mirrors and Lenses* (Ladybird Books Ltd)

† *Simple Science Experiments* by Albert James (Schofield and Sims Ltd)

† *375 Things to do in Science and Nature* by Challand and Brant (Odhams)

† *Science from Toys* published on behalf of the Schools Council by MacDonald Educational

Who might help

Scout Leaders
Venture Scouts
Fathers of Cub Scouts
Science teachers at school

Planning

Science can play a part in Pack Meetings, adding interest to many traditional activities. Models made in a handcraft session can be made to work by applying simple scientific knowledge. Many conjuring tricks rely not so much on sleight of hand as on a principle of science. A puppet theatre could have stage lighting added when a Cub Scout has found out about bulbs and batteries. So science in the Pack is not carried out as a series of work cards, as it might be done in school, but by using the knowledge either gained at school or discovered in the Pack for various realistic situations.

Putting it over

Make a paddle steamer or a cotton reel tank driven by a rubber band—think about springs and tension.
Make a glider. Discover how it flies best.
Have a 'jet-balloon' race—think about jet propulsion.

Make a milk bottle xylophone—think about sound waves.
Make a cigar box guitar with strings—adjust the sounds.
Make a model lighthouse, with a flashing light that works.
Install footlights in your puppet theatre.
Make a pop-gun—and consider how this relates to a petrol pump in a car.
Make a 'Kelly' toy—and find out about gravity.
Make a model railway signal worked by an electro-magnet.
Make a training aid which will switch on a light or sound a buzzer when the right answer is indicated on the board.

Use invisible inks in a special Pack Meeting.
Magnetise a needle and check with a compass that it points to the north.
Make periscopes and use them to find out some secret information in a wide game.
Make a pin-hole camera—and work out why the picture is upside down. Try out a real camera.
Make a 'Cartesian Diver'—discover how divers and submarines stay on the bottom of the sea.

Sense Training

Training aids

Books

* *Cub Scout Games* (The Scout Association)
Books on the life of B.-P.

Who might help

Other Leaders in the Group

Planning

B.-P. always laid great stress on training boys to be alert and quick to notice the small details often overlooked by others, and all his life practised these ideas.
Sight, hearing, taste, smell, touch—our five senses—can all be developed through activities and games, and we can add to these a sixth: common sense. Some people's jobs depend on their ability to detect a slight change in a familiar pattern. Danger is often detected by a smell of burning, or an unfamiliar sound. Much of our pleasure is derived from a keen ear to appreciate music or bird song; or be able to see a sunset or a picture; smell flowers, or enjoy a variety of foods.
A person who is really alert will also be quick to observe when a 'good turn' needs doing, because they will be sensitive to the needs of others.

Putting it over

Sight *Cardboard Chute* Drop a collection of odds and ends down a cardboard mailing tube into a box, leaving a gap of not less than a foot between the two. When all the articles

have been dropped down the chute, the Sixes write down the names of those things they spotted and can remember as they passed the gap.
Detective Invite a friend, who is unknown to the Pack, to visit you for a few minutes during the meeting. Five minutes after he has gone one of the Assistants brings a message, supposedly from the police, asking if a stranger has been seen in the area,

and if so, requiring a full description. Get each Six to give a description. Then invite your friend back into the room for them to check their descriptions.
Advertisements From well-known advertisements cut out the name of the product, and display these as a competition, to see how many the boys can identify.
It happened like this Go out for a short walk round headquarters, asking the Cubs to observe all they see. Arrange with the Troop, or Unit, to stage an incident. Back in your

headquarters, find out how much the Cubs can remember—the colour, make and registration number of a parked car; the time by the church clock; the clothes people were wearing; any suspicious behaviour they saw. Compare the different versions of the incident. What would happen if this was a real case? How correct is the evidence given in Court? What affects the opinions of the various people involved?

Hearing Drop a few selected objects just outside a door. The Pack try to identify the sounds made.

Four people, disguising their voices, read the same paragraph from a book. The Pack, their backs turned or blindfolded, try and identify the readers.

Tape record some of the television advertisement 'jingles' but omit the name of the product. This makes a popular competition.

Tape record some of the familiar sounds of your area: the church bells ringing, the town clock striking, a bus changing gear, the cash till being operated, the door of headquarters closing, Akela's door bell being rung. Use this as a quiz or Six competition.

Obtain from long-term hospital patients a list of some of the sounds about the town they would like to hear and try to produce a tape of their requests. It might include the sounds in the market on Saturday, a pet budgerigar talking, a church choir singing, or some of the items listed previously.

Smell Test a sense of smell by producing fairly familiar scents in bottles or saucers. Do not include ammonia or similar unpleasant ones. Try coffee, cocoa, soap, curry powder, tomato sauce, an orange.

Collect a few flowers with very definite scents and see how many the blindfold Cubs can identify.

Taste Line up some food which the blindfolded Cubs taste and try to identify: sugar, jam, mashed potato, soup, lemonade, yoghurt, etc. Again, do not include unpleasant tastes as this can be upsetting to the players even though it may amuse the organisers of the game. Or make the game more difficult by using a variety of breakfast cereals. Or try a variety of soft drinks, or ice creams.

Have plenty of plastic spoons to use for tasting.

Touch Pass round a bag filled with a variety of objects: a coin, a screw, a paper clip, a small plastic toy, a used match, a wrapped sweet. When all the Six have handled the bag, remove it and let them write down as many articles as they can remember.

Firemen The Cubs remove their shoes, caps, woggles and scarves and jerseys, fold them neatly, and lie on the floor beside them. The light is then put out, and when the leader shouts 'Fire' the firemen must grab their clothes—which have now become helmets, asbestos suits, etc.—and in the dark put them on as fast as they can. After a short time the leader calls 'The fire engine is leaving' and then puts on the light to to check how many firemen were properly dressed.
Pinning on the tail Pin up a picture of Shere Khan and let everyone see it. Then each boy in turn is led blindfold to the picture and given a paper tail which he pins on to the picture as near to the correct position as he can.
Blindfold trail A rope is strung out for the Cubs to hold on to and follow while blindfold. At intervals along it are hung various objects which they must recognise: a couple of sausages, a holly leaf, a rubber spider, and so on. If the game is played in camp in old clothes, the trail can lead them under a fence, through a stream, round a bush or include other suitable hazards which greatly add to the boys' enjoyment.

Service

Training aids

Book

† *Activities for Cub Scouts* (Gilwell Park)

Who might help

Local clergy or doctors may be able to help you find people in need of help
Home Helps, District Nurses
Parents

Planning

Service is not a subject with immediate appeal to a Cub Scout unless it is put over to him in an imaginative way. He may feel the leader is planning his life for him as a round of cleaning shoes, making beds, washing-up and running errands, which is enough to deter any boy from ever being of service to others.

It is helpful if a boy can be involved in a Pack good turn fairly early in his career as a Cub, especially if it is fun: something like an expedition to a camp site to help the Warden.

Gradually he will learn that there is pleasure in giving as well as in receiving, but we must not expect too much from youngsters. Many adults find it hard to do unattractive jobs willingly for other people.

Train the Cubs to carry out the Arrow Badge skills competently: knowing how to use the telephone, to deliver a message correctly, clean a pair of shoes, wash up and make a hot drink: also to be observant and conscientious: they can all be used to help other people. No one will be pleased with the good turn which creates work clearing up the mess afterwards.

Time your Pack good turns at intervals throughout the year. Many elderly people's Homes or children's Homes are inundated with offers of help at Christmas but would welcome a visit to cheer up the dark winter days.

Don't always try to get into the limelight with a press report about a Pack good turn: sometimes it is right to encourage secrecy to develop the attitude of doing a good turn with no thought of praise or reward.

Many ideas which begin with a bang, fizzle out as enthusiasm dwindles. This can have disastrous effect on recipients who might be relying on a weekly visit or some regular service. It is better not to promise too much at the outset.
'Courtesy is the carpet on life's floor,' it is said, and the way in which help is offered and given is as important as the service itself. At the Gold Arrow stage a small act of kindness carried out cheerfully, willingly and faithfully, is better than aiming at a spectacular job which will become a drudgery. It is important for leaders to help boys develop an attitude of courtesy in everyday life, as well as an awareness of the responsibility each of us has in community service and helping those less fortunate than ourselves.

Putting it over

Suggestions for the whole Pack:
Offer the services of the older Cub Scouts as 'ball-boys' at a tennis tournament.
Take an elderly person's weekly washing to the launderette on a rota system.
Plant bulbs in small bowls and present to 'house-bound' people in the neighbourhood, or to friends of the Pack: Group Secretary, badge examiner, caretaker.
Put on a simple show or a puppet play for local 'Over Sixties' Club or 'Darby and Joan Club'.
Give a party for the younger brothers and sisters of Cub Scouts: get the Sixers' Council to suggest suitable games and activities, and involve them in the planning.
Organise a 'work-day' at the District camp site in conjunction with the Camp Warden. Make arrangements beforehand, as the Cubs do not like to be kept waiting to be told what to do: have a change of jobs at intervals. Suitable light jobs might be: acting as a team of carriers of tools or equipment to the Service Team on the site, clearing obstructions from a stream, clearing twigs from a site, picking up litter, helping to stock shelves in the Camp Shop.
Be responsible for keeping part of the churchyard free of weeds for a year. One Six responsible each month.
Make a bird table and arrange to instal it in front of the window of an old people's Home. Keep it supplied with food daily.
For the individual:
Clean the shoes for the whole family for a week.
Clean the bicycle of a younger brother or sister.

Read a bedtime story to a younger child.
Tidy up toys and books after a younger brother or sister, instead of leaving it for Mum to do.
Help older members of the family by fetching and carrying when they are doing a job: car repairs, household repairs or gardening.
Read to an invalid or elderly person.
Make a 'get-well' card for someone who is ill.
Run messages for an elderly neighbour, arranging to call at a regular time each week.
Change library books for a sick person.
Lay the table each day.
Clean Dad's tools after he has had a day in the garden.
Be responsible for keeping the interior of the family car clean, or the wheels and hub caps, which Dad may not be able to reach as easily as a Cub can!
Wash out the paint brushes thoroughly at school.
Tidy books and stack paper neatly in classroom.
Offer to carry things for teachers, caretakers or canteen staff, or open doors for them to pass through if they have their arms full.
Make a telephone call for an elderly person, who may be a little afraid of the telephone having never been taught to use it correctly.
Open car doors and allow older people to get in first.
Write a letter to a relative or friend and pass on family news.
Thoughts for the leader: The importance of example in the habit of service. Cheerfulness, helpfulness, politeness are all infectious qualities. Encourage the Cubs to smile and be courteous to people who serve them in shops, the library or on the bus. Service is not just helping other people, but helping them cheerfully and willingly.
Tell the story of the unknown Scout's 'Good Turn' to publisher William Boyce, which resulted in the spread of Scouting to America.

The Sky at Night

Training aids

Books

* *The Night Sky* (Ladybird Books Ltd)
The Stars and their Legends (Ladybird Books Ltd)

† *Legends of the Stars* by Patrick Moore (Odhams Books Ltd)

† *Stories of the Stars* by Denise Vale (G. Bell & Sons)
* *Signpost to the Stars* (Geo Philip & Son Ltd)
* *Stars at a Glance* (Geo Philip & Son Ltd)

Star Charts

The Daily Telegraph publishes monthly star charts which are very useful.

Who might help

Any adult with an interest in the sky at night and enough patience to help Cub Scouts at beginner's level.

Planning

When the Arrow badge requirements were amended in 1972 there was a general request from leaders to drop 'stars and clouds' from the Arrow Scheme, but investigations showed that this was not because the Cub Scouts were not interested in them, but because of our British weather. It is impossible to rely on the skies to produce either clouds or stars on the Pack night when little Johnny wants to pass his test!

So boys who find this subject interesting can work on a project about the sky at night. This will also allow them to discover rather more than the basic three constellations previously suggested, and perhaps to encourage the development of a new hobby.

Although some work can be done indoors, this is mainly an outdoor activity with an adult who can turn up at short notice when the stars are shining. 'Star-gazing' might form a rather special activity for the older boys on a Pack Holiday or in camp when the younger ones have gone to bed. For city boys this might be the only occasion when they can look up at the stars without street lights spoiling the view. Warm clothing, a torch and a reference book are all that is required, although a pair of binoculars or a telescope will greatly increase the enjoyment. A hot drink in a flask may be welcome too.

Putting it over

Visit the London Planetarium.

Make a planetarium from an old umbrella.

Plot the positions of one constellation at different times of the night, and different seasons of the year. Find out how this happens.

Show how to navigate by the Pole Star.

Make a 'Sky at Night' training aid Cover a large board with black felt or brushed nylon. Cut out stars from thickish cardboard and back each piece with sandpaper. These can then be stuck on the board in the shape of one of the constellations, and coloured. When that constellation can be identified in the sky, another one can be added and a different colour used.

The word 'constellation' in most languages other than English means 'star picture'. Our ancestors saw pictures in the sky, and the stories they told about them have been passed down over the ages. Tell some of these stories at Pack Meetings.

Make a starscope from a washing-up liquid bottle.

Find out what constellations can be seen in the Southern Hemisphere, and which ones well-known to us cannot be seen there.

Find out about the planets, and the moon, and the 'Milky way'

Make a scrap book of any discoveries made.

Swimming

Training aids

Books

- *How to Swim and Dive* (Ladybird Books Ltd)

* *Know the Game—Swimming* (Educational Productions Ltd)
† *Activities for Cub Scouts* (Gilwell Park)

Leaflets, posters etc.

Leaflets, posters, picture quizzes etc., are produced by The Royal Society for the Prevention of Accidents (RoSPA), Saftey Education Division, Cannon House, The Priory Queensway, Birmingham B4 6BS.

Who might help

Members of Amateur Swimming Association
Instructors at local Swimming Pools
Teachers responsible for swimming at local schools
Suitably qualified adult members of the Movement

Planning

To try to get every Cub Scout to be able to swim as soon as possible is part of our adult responsibility, and has little to do with 'passing tests'. The drowning statistics each year make it obvious how vulnerable boys are to this type of accident, mainly because they are so adventure-seeking and unaware of danger at this age. So for his own safety, and perhaps to help others, we should make an all-out effort to get every Cub Scout swimming as early as possible in his time with the Pack.

But this does require an effort, not only by the Pack Scouters but by the Group Scout Leader, Assistant District Commissioner (Cub Scouts) and parents in order to arrange facilities, transport or supervision. Some Packs live so far away from swimming baths or other safe water that regular visits are almost impossible, but for such Packs it is more important than ever that day expeditions are arranged two or three times a year to places where boys can complete the water confidence tests.

Leaders should use qualified instructors where possible to teach the Cubs to swim, but even so the responsibility remains with the leader to ensure that the safety rules are strictly observed.

Where a large number of boys are in the swimming party, it is wise to introduce the 'buddy' system: each boy is paired off with another boy of the same swimming ability. They are expected to stay together and to keep a watch on each other. Every five minutes a whistle is blown and 'buddies' get together and raise their hands—this gives a speedy check for the leaders. Water activities which can be played with the 'buddy'

system will increase the boys' confidence and their swimming ability.
(See also notes under 'Water Safety')

Putting it over

Games for shallow water to help increase confidence.
Lighthouse relay The Cub Scouts line up opposite their 'buddies'. The first boy is given a lighted candle, and on the signal he must race across the pool and hand it over to his partner, who returns with the candle to the starting side. If the candle goes out the boy must go back to the side he set out from to have it re-lit.
Balloon Knock A rope is stretched lengthways down the pool, and the boys line up facing one another, a yard out from the edge, this is marked by a string. Each pair has a balloon. The object of the game is to get the balloon behind the opponent's back marker string to score a goal.
Games to help boys get used to putting their heads underwater.
Egg and spoon race This can be played as a two-man relay race with the Cubs holding the spoon in their hands, or between their teeth. Use pottery eggs if you want them to duck under the water to retrieve any dropped eggs, or ping pong balls if you want dropped balls to float.
Treasure Hunt Wrap some boiled sweets very tightly in aluminium foil, and just before the end of the swimming period scatter them into the water. The Cubs may eat any which they retrieve. (Make sure all are cleared before you leave.)
Ducking tag One Cub Scout is a pelican who is fishing; the

other boys are fish. The only way to avoid being caught is to duck under the water.

Drag race 'Buddies' line up together on one side of the pool and, on the given signal, one boy holds the other boy's hands and walking backwards himself drags his partner across to the other side, where they change over for the return.

Problems: Some boys may be found to have such an innate fear of water that they will not be able to enjoy or respond to such games and activities.

The leader's attitude may have a tremendous influence on these Cubs. Nobody should be allowed to laugh at them; patience, tact and understanding are necessary.

Simple experiments indoors may help to convince boys that the air in their lungs must help them to float: try blowing bubbles down a straw into the bottom of a glass or jam jar; try holding an inflated balloon at the bottom of a bath; play water games with various inflated or semi-inflated objects. Get the boy to think about the control of air and its inevitable buoyancy, which he may remember the next time he goes into the water.

Trails

Training aids

Books

† *Activities for Cub Scouts* (Gilwell Park)

Who might help

Venture Scouts or Patrol Leaders

Planning

Most Cub Scouts enjoy following trails. Besides being an exciting activity, it can provide training in observation and deduction, if tracking signs are properly used.

It is best to begin with easy trails and obvious clues; then to introduce tracking signs, and later more difficult clues, such as a matchstick pushed into a leaf at eye level, a holly leaf on a tree with a very different type of foliage, acorns scattered far from an oak tree. But these signs are easily missed and there must be adequate supervision to prevent anyone going too far astray.

As a general rule the signs should be laid at regular intervals about twenty paces apart, and kept to the same side of the path; sticks and pebbles arranged in the centre of a footpath may get kicked aside unintentionally by other passers-by.
If a large group is following the same trail, start the Cubs at timed intervals otherwise all the excitement will be gained by a few who run on ahead, while slower boys will just follow after them rather than look for signs. Alternatively have a separate trail for each Six, all meeting together at the end.
Take care not to leave litter. You may wish to use silver foil (as jewels spilt by the robbers as they make a fast get-away), or strands of wool (torn from the robbers' clothing), or large paper footprints (to be found by explorers looking for the abominable snowman), and if so these should be counted to ensure that all the pieces are collected. Points might be awarded to those boys who collect most; even so, a Scouter should bring up the rear to collect any pieces which have been missed.

Putting it over

All observation games are good training for Cubs. But there are several specialized games which can be used indoors in preparation for following out-door trails.
Pelmanism A set of cards is prepared, half of them showing the various tracking signs and the other half with the names or descriptions of the signs. The players sit in a circle and the cards are spread out face down in the centre. The first player turns up two cards, and shows the other players what they are. If they are a pair, (i.e. a sign and its corresponding name) he keeps them. If not he replaces them exactly where they were and everyone must try to remember them. Subsequently players turn up one card, and pause to remember or guess where the corresponding card is, before turning up the second card. If a player turns up a 'pair' he has a second turn. The player with most pairs at the end is the winner. It is best to start with about 16 cards, and a set for each Six is preferable.
Six Relay In front of each Six is placed a pile of pebbles, sticks and grass. The players are numbered. The leader calls out the name of a tracking sign and the number of a Cub, who must collect some material from the pile and run to the far end of the room and lay out the correct sign. Each player who makes the correct sign within 10 seconds scores a point for his team.
Tell a story of some boys who followed a trail, mentioning the various signs they passed on the way. As each sign is

mentioned the members of each Six take it in turn to draw the correct sign on a large sheet of paper.

Out of doors Stories may be used to add zest to out-door activities too. A burglar in a smash and grab raid might be badly cut by glass and leave a trail of blood. By following the trail detectives may be able to find his hide-out and the stolen jewellery (sweets). A mixture of red poster paint and scouring powder makes good 'blood' sprinkled at intervals; but remembering that these horrific things must be cleared up or covered over at the end of the game.

A good turn trail A card is given to the Cubs working on this, on which is written: 'Help! Follow trail'. Remember to lay the trail beforehand. At the end the 'help' required might be a genuine 'good turn'— weeding a garden, clearing litter, or whatever can be suitably arranged, and maybe described in a hidden message.

Laying a trail A small group of older boys are told that some 'foreign' Cub Scouts are visiting the Pack and as they speak no English the only way to guide them from the bus stop to the headquarters is to lay a trail of tracking signs. The 'foreign' Cub Scouts could be a neighbouring Pack arriving for a joint meeting (they will have miraculously learnt to speak English by the time they arrive!).

Activity trail A trail is set out using tracking signs with messages left at intervals for activities which can be done at each place. ('Draw the tree's leaf', 'sketch this gate', 'identify this flower', 'find three different types of grass growing here'.)

The Sixes set off at intervals and receive points for the best time and the most activities satisfactorily completed.

Visits

Training aids

Books

Discovering English Customs and Traditions by Margaret Gascoine (Shire Publications)
This is one of a list of titles in the 'Discovering' Series which gives many ideas for expeditions based on places and customs in England, and gives the dates when the traditional ceremonies take place.

I-Spy Series (Dickens Press)

In the Street
On the Road
Sights of London
Churches
Signs and Symbols
Buses and Coaches
History
On a Car Journey
On a Train Journey

Ladybird Series (Ladybird Books Ltd)

Church and Cathedrals
Houses and Homes
Lighthouses
Lightships and Lifeboats
* *London*
* *Understanding Maps*

Local Guide books or resource books appropriate to venue or activity.

† *Out and About*—A guide to safety on educational visits. Published for the Schools Council by Evans/Methuen Educational Press.

† *Activities for Cub Scouts* (Gilwell Park)

Who might help

Obviously you must obtain the co-operation of the curators, wardens, vergers, managers, or whoever is in charge of the place you intend to visit. This should be done well beforehand, by a personal visit if possible, followed up by a letter confirming all the details.
Parents, with transport, would be invaluable, especially if they would help to take care of small groups of boys during the visit.

Planning

The places Cub Scouts will enjoy visiting will depend on their environment. A town Pack would enjoy a visit to a farm, but

the country Pack may prefer to visit an airport or a museum or a railway station.
The more you are able to involve the Pack in the plans the more interested they will be on the day of the visit. Include activities in the previous meetings which are a preparation for the visit. Prepare some quiz sheets for use on the day.
Plan well ahead, keep parents fully informed. Take adequate adult help. Carry a first-aid kit. Have alternative plans for wet weather. Avoid long, tedious journeys and potential hazards. Include a short rest period sometime during the day: the leaders will need it even if the Cubs don't!
Remember that the general public tends to judge the whole Movement by what it sees of any individual section, so ensure that the appearance of everyone in your party is clean and smart and that all behave in a courteous and considerate manner towards members of the public and to each other. Nothing gets the Movement a bad name faster than a Pack of ill-behaved, scruffy boys, and leaders who allow them to be so.

Putting it over

These are some of the places which Cub Scouts have enjoyed visiting and no doubt you can add your own ideas to the list:—
In the country: a farm; stables; nature reserve; zoo; camp site.

Places connected with history: a church, with a tower to climb; a cathedral; museums, particularly transport museums; castles, particularly ones with dungeons; walk round old city walls; windmill.

To watch things being made: boat builder's yard; blacksmith's shop; pottery; sweet factory; toy factory; soft drinks factory; weaving mill; bakery; printing works.
Places and people who provide a public service: telephone exchange; fire station; police station; signal box; lifeboat station; lighthouse; accident prevention exhibitions.
Sport to watch or play: a football match; a cricket match; a swimming pool; the beach.
Transport: an airport; a harbour; docks; a railway station; engine sheds; ride on a canal boat; traction engine rally; ride on a hovercraft; ride on a train, bus or the underground (still exciting to some boys who travel mostly by car).

Water Safety

Training aids

The Royal Society of the Prevention of Accidents, Saftey Education Division, Cannon House, The Priory Queensway, Birmingham B4 6BS, has an extensive range of material on this, perhaps one of the most important subjects. Details of prices are available upon request. Much of the material below is produced by them.

Books

* *The Story of Lighthouses* (Ladybird Books Ltd)
* *Lightships and Lifeboats* (Ladybird Books Ltd)
* *The Lifeboat Men* (Ladybird Books Ltd)
My Country and Seaside Safety Book—SE30
The Code for Water Safety—WS12

Cards

The National Code for Bathers—WS6

Charts

Spot the Dangers—WS11—picture quiz
Water can be dangerous—WSP13-1
Learn Water Sense—WSP10-5
Swim where it is safe—WSP14-3
Swim Safely—SP39—A SCOUTING Magazine Training chart. Available from the Editorial Department of Headquarters.

Leaflets

Learn the Water Safety Rules—WS44—A fold-out leaflet about the dangers of canals, rivers, gravel pits, etc. Advice when swimming, fishing, canoeing in a 'fill in the word' exercise.

Learn Water Sense—WS2—A fold-out leaflet about what to do when you or someone else falls in the water and advice on sea bathing. Another 'fill in the missing word' exercise.

Train for Safety—WS4—This contains details of swimming awards for children in primary schools.

Who might help

The Royal Society for the Prevention of Accidents—for resource material
Local Accident Prevention Officer
Local Swimming Club
Qualified first-aider to teach mouth-to-mouth resuscitation
Lifeboat station

Planning

To most Cub Scouts, water means adventure. They love to swim in it, play in it, sail boats on it, fish in it, go in boats on it, and if it freezes, walk on it. Unfortunately, the water that brings so much fun can also bring tragedy. In the United Kingdom almost 1,000 people are accidentally drowned each year. The 5-9 year age group is most at risk. 75% of drowning accidents occur in inland waters.

It is clear from this that Cub Scout leaders have a real opportunity to help in the work of accident prevention. The aim should be to train every boy to swim and to be able to perform life-saving techniques, so as to safeguard himself and other people from injury or loss of life. Marking off a feather in *the Cub Programme Booklet* is only a subsidiary to this real target of self-preservation and the ability to help others who might get into difficulties in water.

Putting it over

Make posters illustrating any of the Water Safety Rules. Arrange for them to be hung in your headquarters for a month.

Make a series of charts on the National Code for Bathers. If you live on the coast, perhaps they could be exhibited during a major holiday period to remind the general public to take care near the sea.

Arrange for someone to show the Pack how to use a lifebelt. Allow the Cubs to try throwing it, and see how many can reach a given target.

Arrange a life-saving demonstration at the local swimming baths. Encourage good swimmers in your Pack to work for the Rescuer badge.

Visit a lifeboat, or inshore rescue boat, station.

Artificial resuscitation. Arrange for qualified instruction on a 'Resusci-Annie' or similar model. Don't be satisfied until all the adults who help with the Pack are competent, and many of the boys should be able to carry it out successfully.

Compose a song based on the Water Safety Rules, to the tune of 'Ten Green Bottles', teach it to the Pack.

Have a Water Safety Quiz.

Each Six to mime a story including a possible water hazard: children playing near a gravel pit; family on holiday on a canal boat; boys fishing in a pond when line gets tangled with reeds; a small girl gets out of her depth at a swimming pool.

Carry out a beach survey if you live by the sea. Find out what accidents occur on your beach. The First Aid Post may be able to give you statistics, also how they were caused: drifting out on an air bed, throwing pebbles, going after a beach ball drifting out to sea, going in a dinghy without a life-jacket, broken glass—the result of leaving litter.

Run an 'Aquanaut Campaign'. To qualify as an aquanaut a Cub Scout must show that he respects the water, masters it and enjoys it. This is one of the goals of 10-year-old boys in the Boy Scouts of America. To show that he respects water, a boy must understand that water can be dangerous and never take foolish risks, or break the water safety rules. To show mastery of the water implies learning to swim really well, and to be able to carry out rescue techniques. To enjoy water a boy will have so developed his skills that he can go on to be a snorkeler and discover the fascination of underwater swimming,

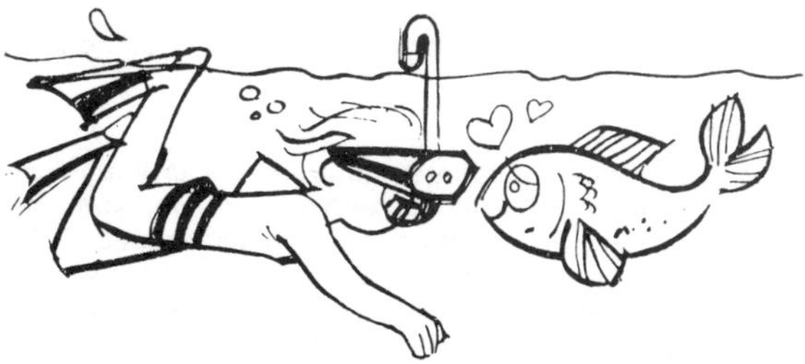

or a dinghy sailor or canoeist knowing what to do if he capsizes.

Make a Pack 'Safe Depth' Chart. Make a chart showing three areas of water; one marked 'Not over $3\frac{1}{2}$ feet deep' for those who cannot swim; one $3\frac{1}{2}$ to 6 feet for those who can swim at least 50 ft., and the last one from 6 ft. to 12 ft. for those who can swim 100 yards or more. Cut out some figures of boys in plain white paper, give one to each boy on which to write his name. He then sticks his 'paper boy' to the chart with a pin in the appropriate area. As his ability increases he can move his 'boy' to the next area.

(See also the section on Swimming).

Plan a Meeting on the theme of Lifeboats.

Come dressed in sou-westers and wellingtons.

Make a model lifeboat.

Act a rescue at sea. A Cub Scout leader acts as television interviewer afterwards—'What do you feel like?'

Play 'Port and Starboard'.

Game—'Crossing the Line'—Group Scout Leader as King Neptune.

'What things sink' activity (don't test Akela!).

Good turn—raise funds for R.N.L.I.

Sing a sea shanty.

Yarn—a sea story.

Prayers—for volunteer lifeboat men.

Weather

Training aids

Books

- * *Weather* (Ladybird Books Ltd)
- † *375 Things to do in Science and Nature*—Challand and Brandt (Odhams)
- * *Know the Game—Weather* (Educational Productions Ltd)

Who might help

Find out where weather recordings are made in your area. The officials there might be able to help you, or perhaps the staff at the museum, an R.A.F. Station or a civil aerodrome.

The science teacher at school.

A farmer or sailor or other person who makes a habit of noting weather conditions because it affects their job.

Planning

From earliest times men have looked for signs and indications of the weather to come. Many of the old rhymes about weather-lore, handed down to us over the ages, have a lot of truth in them, as they were based on the observation of the weather over many years:

Red sky at night,
Shepherd's delight'.

Today the Meteorological Office bases its forecasts on scientifically recorded facts, but even so it does not give detailed forecasts for more than 24 hours ahead, as in the British Isles we know only too well that our weather can never be depended upon.

Cub Scouts enjoy building their own weather stations and taking readings, and even a simple knowledge of some of the weather signs will be found useful. If a Cub can recognise a nimbo-stratus cloud, or the huge cumulus cloud often called an anvil, he may save himself getting soaked by taking a raincoat with him on outings, because he knows these are rain clouds.

Putting it over

An ideal time for carrying out a Pack project on the weather is at a Pack Holiday or camp, when readings can be taken on several consecutive days. A build-up to the 'weather-camp' can take place over several weeks previously and everyone can be involved in the building of simple apparatus. You may even find yourself hoping for a wet day just to give some different readings!

Make an anemometer for measuring the speed of the wind.

Draw a Beaufort Scale chart showing the signs to be observed at different wind speeds.

Make a barometer for measuring the air pressure.

Construct a wind vane.

Make a rain gauge.

Measure the temperature, using a maximum and minimum thermometer if possible, and record this on a chart.

Use cotton wool or polystyrene to make a pictorial chart showing the three main types of clouds, their form, their height and the weather they indicate.

Details of how to make these simple pieces of apparatus will be found in the books listed above.

Develop a wall frieze to show pictures of all the people whose jobs are dependent on the weather: a farmer judging the right time to make hay, a steeple-jack unable to climb too high in

windy weather, an airline pilot grounded by fog, a lifeboat man needing skill and courage to brave storms at sea, a driver of a high-sided transporter unable to journey along open motorways in strong winds, or Scouts hoping it will not be too windy when they pitch their tents.

Wide Games

Who might help

Other Scouters in the Group

Venture Scouts
Fathers of Cub Scouts

Planning

'Wide Games' is the traditional name given to outdoor adventurous games played over a wide area of land, normally with some cover. The game is often built round an exciting story which appeals to the Cub Scouts' love of make-believe. This is the kind of activity which boys expect when they join the Pack and most enjoy. Yet many leaders do not look for the opportunity for wide games. They may demand rather more effort to organise than a normal Pack activity, particularly if one lives in a city, but whatever the details of the plan, as a general rule the pleasure they give to the Cubs is well worth the trouble.

Whatever the details of the plan, as a general rule, the Leader should:

have clearly defined boundaries which the Cubs most know;

have simple rules which are easy to understand;

devise the game so that everyone runs towards a central base rather than chases indefinitely over a wide area. In their excitement boys may get lost, unless the game is planned so that they gradually move from the boundaries towards the centre;

ensure that the starting and finishing signals will be audible and/or visible over the whole area, and that the final rallying point is a well-known or conspicuous landmark;

have plenty of adult help available, a minimum of three is advisable even for the smallest of Packs;

have some method of re-entering the game if caught, by paying a penalty or answering a question, rather than being eliminated

count heads at the end of the game to ensure that no one is lost.

Putting it over

The theme for the story may be suggested by the type of country which is to be used: wooded, open or hilly country, or containing some special feature like a river or bridge. If these should present a hazard, the wide game must be planned accordingly and the adult help strategically placed.

Wide games of a different sort may be used in urban or suburban areas. These call for more imagination and forethought on the part of the leaders, but opportunities do arise and should not be ignored.

In a suburban area
The following potted stories might be used for the theme:
Scoop
The newspaper which prints a story first sells the most copies, and so the reporters working for any one paper will try and get a story to their Editor before those working for rival papers can hit the headlines.
Each Six has a page from a different newspaper torn into about a dozen pieces. All but two of the Six are reporters and have to carry the story from the scene of the event to the Editor's office, one piece at a time. The other two from each Six try to intercept the reporters who must hand over the pieces they are carrying if caught.
International Congress
Representatives of several countries have met together to work out a new world currency system and because this involves them in difficult mathematical calculations they have said that no reporters or television cameras will be allowed in the room. However, to keep the world informed they will publish bulletins at intervals, giving the rate of exchange for each country as it is fixed. No words will be used in the message only flags and figures so that everyone can understand it—e.g. 8/1 followed by the flag of the United States of America, thus there will be 8 American dollars to one new pound.

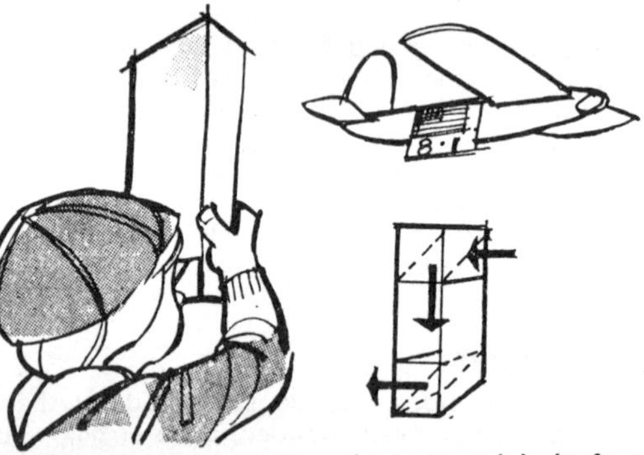

Unfortunately once the congress has started it is found that the room window is too high for anyone to see through so each Six must first make a periscope in order to be able to read the messages. Each boy in turn looks through the window using the periscope and reads one of the messages and memorises the flag. A book or chart of flags must be available so that any which are unknown can be checked.

To add to the fun the message could be written on a piece of paper, attached to a balsa wood glider and launched to take the news overseas, to where the Sixer is waiting to make a full list of all the rates of exchange.

In the Country

Potted stories which might form the basis of wide games.

Medical Mission Each Six is a medical mission team trying to get valuable life-saving drugs (sweets) across the jungle swamp to the hospital (staffed by Akela) at the centre. Unfortunately the swamp is the hunting ground of many ferocious animals (other assistants and helpers), who snatch the drugs from any person they catch, and the runners must then return to their base for a further supply. Drugs can only be carried one packet at a time.

Ascent of Everest Each Six is a climbing party attempting to reach the summit of the snow-capped mountain (marked by a block of polystyrene guarded by the abominable snowman in the guise of Akela). Each party has a small flag and a collection of equipment required on the expedition: a pencil, adhesive plaster, compass, pack of dried food, etc. The aim is to get as much equipment as possible to the 'summit'.

Various hazards exist en route: blizzards, avalanches, snow-storms (the assistants), which are liable to break the piece of wool round each climber's arm. If they succeed the climber himself becomes a 'hazard' and helps to catch the others. The winners are the party with most pieces of their equipment on the summit, but the most important piece of all is the flag, for if that is missing the party cannot claim to have conquered the peak.

Yarns

Training aids

Newspapers, magazines, radio, television and one's own experiences, all provide material for short stories which can be turned into five-minute yarns for the Pack. The children's section of the public library can also be a valuable source of inspiration. There are so many books available for children today that it is impossible to list them all, however, these are, perhaps, some of the best.

Books

*† *The Cub Scout Annual* (World International Publishing Ltd)

*† *The International Cub Scout Book* (World International Publishing Ltd)

The Jungle Book by Rudyard Kipling (Macmillan & Co Ltd)

The Second Jungle Book by Rudyard Kipling (Macmillan & Co Ltd)

All the Mowgli Stories by Rudyard Kipling (Macmillan & Co Ltd)

Kim by Rudyard Kipling (Macmillan & Co Ltd)

† *A Storyteller's Choice* by Eileen Colwell (Bodley Head Press)—a selection of stories with notes on how to tell them

† *Legends of the Stars* by Patrick Moore (Odhams)

† *Stories of the Stars* by Denise Vale (G. Bell & Sons Ltd)

*† *The Outdoor Adventure Book* (World International Publishing Ltd.)

Who might help

A local librarian who could help with the selection of suitable books and, perhaps, tips on storytelling as many children's libraries have 'Story-Time' clubs
The Assistant District Commissioner (Cub Scouts)
Group Scout Leader
Scout Leader
Vicar or Minister

Planning

If you are not used to telling yarns to your Cubs, the following tips may help you to introduce an extra item into your Pack Meetings which the boys will appreciate and thoroughly enjoy, and which can be a most valuable 'tool' in training.

To prepare:

1. Find a story which you enjoy and read it through to get the atmosphere. Choose a short story the first time.
2. Re-read it to fix the 'framework' of it in your mind: the plot, the characters, the sequence of events, the essential points.
3. Tell it to yourself to see how much you can remember.
4. Go back and look up the parts you had forgotten, and try to fix them in your memory.
5. Look for any colourful turn of phrase—vivid descriptions—key words.
6. If helpful, make a few notes and headings on a postcard, but do not depend upon them.
7. Make sure you have a good beginning and a good ending.

On the night:

1. Tell your story—don't be too dramatic and act it. Story-telling is a descriptive art not a dramatic one, so paint the picture with words.
2. Don't hurry—allow for the telling pause which heightens excitement or creates suspense, but never long enough to lose interest.
3. Inflection and the correct use of voice is important.
4. Try and see the action in your mind's eye, and describe it as though it was really happening.
5. Make sure that the Cubs are sitting comfortably, that they can see your face, and you can see theirs, and if a boy is inattentive catch his eye and tell the story directly to him for a while.

Yarns will become one of your most valuable working tools with the Pack if you select them with a purpose in mind: to fit in with the theme of the meeting, to quieten the Pack before going home, to add an element of surprise and fun to the evening, to explore various values and standards, to add colour or understanding to other activities or to emphasize a special occasion.

Putting it over

Stories for Fun Cub Scouts have a keen sense of fun, and laughter unites the Pack in happiness. Such a story can be used to enliven an evening which needs a laugh, to reunite the Pack after some upheaval, to fill an awkward moment, during an unforeseen wait or whilst Akela talks to an unexpected visitor, or to add an element of surprise to a Pack Meeting.

Stories for Special Occasions Have a fund of stories ready for such occasions as Investitures, Going-up Ceremonies, the award of a Proficiency badge on an Act of Worship.

Scientific Stories Older boys in particular delight in hearing of underwater adventures, or explorations in space. Care must be taken to be factually correct where possible, partly because the ten-year olds are quickly growing away from the world of make-believe to the world of reality, and partly because today's youngsters are often more knowledgeable in such technology than adults. In these days too, fiction tends to become fact rather more quickly than we imagined it would—it is not so long ago that a man walking on the moon was a ridiculous flight of fancy!

Nature Yarns, both factual and allegorical, can do much to arouse interest in nature, concern for wild life and a desire to protect rather than destroy. This type of yarn is very useful to set the scene for a Pack conservation project, on expeditions to the country, or to give five minutes rest after eating a picnic meal.

Legends, Mythology and Stories of Heroism These are grouped together only because they are the type of stories which have colour, richness and sometimes profound truth. Boys often see themselves as the hero and unconsciously try to adopt the same fine qualities. Many Bible stories come into this category. Such a story told in the half-light as dusk begins to fade, or when sitting round a campfire, will often cause a boy to appreciate the values and moral standards of life: courage, truth, honesty or unselfishness, much more than any 'straight talk' by a leader would do.

Serial Stories can be used to great effect to give stability to a Pack undergoing a change of leadership, or where attendance is fluctuating. A story told in serial form on successive evenings of a Pack Holiday can have a quietening effect on the Cub Scouts at the end of the day, in readiness for bed.

Stories on the theme on one of the Arrow Activity Areas Watch the newspapers and magazines for short stories or anecdotes to set the scene for a project on home safety, the Country Code, the Royal Family, or on a more general theme for a series of meetings—perhaps 'International Scouting' or 'helping other people'. It is well worth while to keep your own note book of potted yarns. It is easy to forget a story or its source unless you have a ready-reference book.

Ideas to involve the Cub Scouts in story-telling.

Action story Before telling a story, allocate a character or object to each Six or smaller group of boys. As the story proceeds each group stands up, turns round and sits down again, when their 'character' or 'object' is mentioned e.g. in a story about a fairground, one group might be 'roundabouts', another 'staliholders', another 'caravans'. Choose words which occur frequently in the story. Have one word which is a signal for all to get up and turn round—it might be 'fairground' in the story illustrated.

Snowball Yarn You begin a story then each person in turn adds to it. It should have a dramatic flavour in order to 'spark off' everyone's imagination. Preferably with a small group, so that all have a chance to contribute.

How did it end? Look for reports in newspapers which have unusual endings or where two or three different endings could equally well have happened. Tell the first part of the story and ask the Cub Scouts to work out their own version of an ending. Finally, read out what really happened.

Book Readers Some boys who may be interested in this badge, are often of a quieter nature and are apt to be passed over in the hurly-burly of a lively Pack. But they should be encouraged, they might like to tell others something of the theme of an exciting incident in a book they are reading.

Picture Story Find a picture, in a magazine or book, which portrays plenty of action. Show it to the Pack for a few minutes, and then give them five minutes to make up a story telling what they think is happening. One spokesman for each Six then tells their story to the rest of the Pack.

Five Minute Yarns Give each Six a card on which is noted the scene or setting of a story and a list of characters or objects which have to be included in the yarn. After five

DONALD ALLAN

minutes preparation the whole Pack gathers together to hear each yarn in turn.

The cards might include:

Scene:	A supermarket	Characters: & props	The Mayor. A tin of spaghetti. A football. A lady with a broken umbrella. A stick of celery. Young man in a bowler hat.
Scene:	Outside Wembley Stadium on the morning of the Cup Final	Characters: & props	An angry farmer. A Sixer. A tube train. A copy of the Jungle Book. An argumentative duck. A revolving door.
Scene:	A Scout headquarters	Characters: & props	A Frenchman. A fish. Long road uphill. A sixpenny stamp. Roll-top desk with woodworm. A petrol pump attendant.

Hats In the same way each Six can be given one or more objects which they have to work into a story. Such items might be:

A Lady Cub Scout Leader's hat and a ball point pen.

A postman's hat and a packet of salt.

A mountaineer's knitted 'bobble' cap, a bus ticket and a sausage.

A fancy straw hat and a mousetrap.

UNBECOMING BEHAVIOR

KATE COLBY

UGLY DUCKLNG PRESSE

Thank you to the editors of *Aufgabe*, *New American Writing* and *Kadar Koli*, in which sections of this poem first appeared. Thank you also to Russell Kinnicutt, whose advice, vision and support are integral to this work.

First Edition, Ugly Duckling Presse, 2008
ISBN 978-1-933254-40-1

Cataloging-in-publication data is available
from the Library of Congress.

Ugly Duckling Presse
at the Old American Can Factory
232 Third Street, #E-002
Brooklyn, NY 11215
(www.uglyducklingpresse.org)

Distributed by Small Press Distribution
(www.spdbooks.org)

Ugly Duckling Presse is a member of the
Council of Literary Magazines and Presses.

Design/Typesetting: Don't Look Now!
Type: Gill Sans and Garamond
Cover Image: E.G. Lutz, *Practical Drawing*, Scribner, 1922
Cover Printing: PolyprintDesign
Cover Paper: Fabriano
Printing & Binding: McNaughton & Gunn